RIFF, RAM, BAH, ZOO!

FOOTBALL COMES TO TCU

RIFF, RAM, BAH, ZOO!
FOOTBALL COMES TO TCU

EZRA HOOD

With a Foreword by
Coach Gary Patterson

TCU
PRESS

Fort Worth, Texas

Library of Congress Cataloging-in-Publication Data

Hood, Ezra, 1979-

Riff, ram, bah, zoo! : football comes to TCU / Ezra Hood.

    p. cm.

 Includes bibliographical references and index.

1. Texas Christian University--Football--History. 2. Football--
Texas--History. I. Title. II. Title: Football comes to TCU.

GV958.T442H66 2013

796.332'63097645315--dc23

                    2013013637

All photographs unless otherwise noted are courtesy of Special
Collections, Mary Couts Burnett Library, TCU.

TCU Press
P.O. Box 298300
Fort Worth, TX

www.prs.tcu.edu

To order books: 1.800.826.8911

Designed by fusion29.com

FOREWORD

TCU football has a long and proud heritage, and all TCU fans will appreciate *Riff, Ram, Bah, Zoo! Football Comes to TCU*, a rich sports history that chronicles this great legacy. Written by TCU alum Ezra Hood and published by TCU Press, *Riff, Ram, Bah, Zoo!* tells the story of TCU football's first two lively decades, when playing fields were often uneven and rules were sometimes irregular. Although the spirit of the game and the passion of the players haven't changed, the sport certainly has. Without the sophisticated gear of today, TCU's earliest players competed in hand-sewn uniforms, leather helmets, and nose guards on rocky, hard-packed ground with sketchy boundaries, no end zones, and more than a few horned frogs. There were no forward passes, and in the pile of bodies that often ended each play, fans could only distinguish their team from the opponent's by the color of the players' socks. Yet despite opposition from within and without, TCU created its football program in 1896 at a time when many still questioned the value of the new sport. TCU fielded its teams by any means—usually on the first day of the fall semester, when the coaches found out who had shown up to play—or to learn how to play. Since those early years TCU's players and coaches, with the support of thousands of fans, have proudly carried the sport of football forward, earning respect for over a century.

The importance of tradition to our football program cannot be overstated. From the achievements of the "Boys from the Heights" in the team's first year to the triumphs of the team entering the Southwest Conference in 1922, TCU football set the foundation for its gridiron success. I am proud to build on the foundation these coaches and players established one hundred and twenty years ago. I think they would also be proud if they could see all that has been accomplished over the last twelve years. Now the football program is the "front porch" of a great and growing university.

—Coach Gary Patterson, August 2013

ACKNOWLEDGMENTS

Writing about football and about TCU at the turn of the last century is to cope with erasures. Custom all but erased the first names of many players, who were identified only by their last names in most contemporary accounts. I have been able to fill in most of the players' names from the lettermen lists and other sources. But in too many instances the only mention of a player here will be his last name. Perhaps the publication of this book will prompt more of these early players' names and stories to resurface.

Progress erases the setting of many of these stories. Carroll Field now sits under a Baylor University administrative building; West End Park is now a Waco junkyard. It is difficult even for the imaginative to hear the calls and crowds of the games described in these pages when standing in these lots today, generations removed from the bucks and tackles of yesteryear.

But most of all, time erases. In an institution as self-aware as TCU, the fact that the memory of its earliest coaches, games, and players could fade is a testament to the eroding vigor of time. This work grew largely from my curiosity to rediscover the TCU football stories time had erased.

My efforts would not have made it into print without the cooperative effort and sacrifice of many others. This book's journey from harebrained idea to these printed pages was blessed—and occasionally cursed—by many. Of course my editors, Klay Kubiak and Kathy Walton, labored with me to find a printable book amid my manuscripts. The TCU Press gambled on me, and I hope your copy of the book helps them win that gamble. My readers gave valuable feedback early on, and my friends suffered (and suffer!) through my incessant discoveries of arcane trivia about TCU football.

A particular thanks goes to Lisa Pena and Susan Swain of Special Collections in the Mary Couts Burnett Library at TCU. They were an invaluable help in rounding up images for this book.

But mostly I want to leave a public thanks on this page for my dear wife and fellow Horned Frog, Shannon, who spent many a widow's evening during the years I labored on this project, somehow never complaining.

Ezra Hood

1
TCU:
THE BEGINNINGS

The town of Fort Worth, Texas, began in 1849 as a frontier fort that was abandoned by the army four years later, in favor of an outpost farther west. Some of the soldiers stayed behind to settle in the little village that had depended on the fort, including Francis Knaar, a blacksmith, and Louis Wetmore, who cut the fort's first street through waist-high grass. Surprisingly, the village survived, and by 1869, Fort Worth had a stone courthouse surrounded by a grocer, butcher, hardware store, three drugstores, a brickyard, a ferry, a mill, saddlery, cabinet shop, two blacksmith shops, two hotels, a wagon yard, several mercantiles, a law firm, a Masonic Lodge, and a shoe shop. In town, sunflowers grew "as tall as a mule's back,"and razorback hogs ran openly in the streets, fighting with dogs and breeding flies.[1]

Wolves threatened settlers in the early days; as late as 1905 wolf hunts were still attracting hunters—including Teddy Roosevelt—from the East. After the Civil War, the town's school was held in Masonic Lodge Number 148, whose floors had been ripped up to build looms during the war. The building was repaired with lumber that Major Khleber Miller Van Zandt (who had once worked in Abraham Lincoln's law office) and three others had bought for a load of flour.

Captain John Hanna—an ex-Confederate soldier and lawyer—and Carl Vincent taught at the school after the war, drawing students from surrounding counties, as well as from Fort Worth. In 1868, Hanna quit teaching in order to resume his law practice, and Colonel John Peter Smith, who had started a school in 1854, returned to teaching after serving in the Confederate Army. He hired a newlywed schoolteacher from Carlton College in Bonham—the son of Fort Worth Postmaster Joseph Addison Clark. Like John Hanna before him, Smith also retired from teaching so that he could resume his law practice.

Hiring Addison Clark to teach in Fort Worth was something of a coup—the young teacher was more of a scholar than one would expect in as rough a place as Fort Worth. He was the brightest pupil in a family of scholars. After exhausting what education was available to him in Texas, he taught himself Hebrew and Greek. While campaigning with the Confederate Army, Addison read Byron, the Bible, and a work on higher mathematics translated from French. Upon returning from the war, Addison and his brother Randolph, who were very close, went to Bonham and studied with Charles Carlton, who had studied with Alexander Campbell

1

in England. Addison married Carlton's niece, Sally McQuigg; Randolph married a cousin once removed of Robert E. Lee named Ella Branch Lee. Many of the Clarks were teachers, and eventually both Joseph and his wife, as well as four other children, including Randolph, taught with Addison in the Clarks' school. When Addison and Sally had their first child, a son born in 1870, they named him Adran (also spelled Add Ran) Clark—to honor both the father and the uncle.

Addison was an unrepentant Southerner who refused to take the iron-clad oath, but got a teaching certificate anyway. He was also a devout Christian whose devotion to Biblical Christianity soon got him into trouble in Fort Worth. The Masons objected to Clark's preaching in their building on Sundays. When they threatened to oust the school and its preachy schoolmaster, Van Zandt and others bought a lot nearby for $200 and built a forty- by thirty-foot brick building for the school and church.[2] Whether by custom, or foresight, or both, they built a stout fence around the lot, which saved many of the school children from a cattle stampede following an annual May Day picnic. The picnickers heard the cattle coming, and those with carts and buggies rode out of the way. Joseph Clark led the rest—mostly children—back to the school and helped the kids over the fence. One of the cowboys saved Joseph from the stampede by scooping up the teacher and fastening him by his clothes to the saddle horn.

The Clarks' school soon outgrew its two-room schoolhouse. Major Van Zandt and Judge Terry bought a lot on Fourth Street between Houston and Main and gave it to the Christian Church (Disciples of Christ), whose congregants built on it a new building to house both their church and their school. Ida Van Zandt Jarvis boarded female students of the school at her home—the first boarding for female students in Tarrant County.

By 1870, Tarrant County had almost six thoursand inhabitants and over sixteen thousand acres under cultivation, primarily for wheat and cotton. And the cattle trade, which Monroe Choate, J. J. Myers, and J. L. Driskell had largely driven away from Dallas, was transforming the town of Fort Worth. A Kentucky paper editorialized, "Fort Worth is a shabby village on a small river not over ankle deep. . . . The country is sparsely settled, dwellings are five miles apart. But in two years it will be twice the size of Lexington. Fort Worth has a population of two thousand inhabitants. It is having unrivaled growth and ere long will surpass Richmond, Virginia, in population growth."[3]

By the 1870s, Fort Worth not only had rosy prospects, but a reputation as well. Drovers' herds down the Chisholm Trail would take over an hour to pass through town, unless the cowboys settled down for a few days to enjoy city life in "Hell's Half Acre," a cluster of saloons, gambling houses, and other establishments of ill repute that were uncomfortably close to the Clarks' school and church. The deterioration of the neighbor-

Randolph Clark in front of his home, Thorp Spring, 1890.

hood accelerated in 1872, when the Texas and Pacific Railroad contracted to build a railroad from San Diego to East Texas, prompting an influx of newcomers, a building boom, and speculation in real estate.

The situation quickly grew intolerable for the Clarks. Only months after Fort Worth was incorporated as a city, Addison went away for the summer to preach and to look for a new site for the school. Meanwhile, Randolph received an offer from Pleasant Thorp to relocate the school to the sleepy environs of Thorp Spring, a couple of miles outside of Granbury. The area charmed Randolph, and he convinced Joseph and Addison to move their school to Thorp Spring. The three hoped to be able to pay for the school from the proceeds of their Fort Worth homes, which had continued to rise in value until the bubble burst in the Panic of 1873. Little Add Ran, however, had recently died of diphtheria, and Sallie Clark did not wish to move away from her son's grave. She eventually relented when the three men—Joseph, Addison, and Randolph—promised her that they would name the school after the child.

The first session of the "Add Ran" school opened with thirteen pupils from nearby towns. Despite speculation by the locals that it would not last a full term, the little school steadily grew. The Christian Church endorsed the school in December 1873. The Clarks applied for and won a charter from the State of Texas in April 1874, under the name Add Ran Male and Female College, called simply "Add Ran College" for short. By the close of the spring term in 1874, seventy-five students from several counties were enrolled. Primary grade students paid two dollars monthly; intermediate grade students paid three to four dollars monthly, and college students paid five dollars monthly. Add Ran's first graduates were J. E. Jarrott and Edwin Milwee, in June 1876. Enrollment reached two hundred in that year, and leveled out at about four hundred students by the 1881-82 school year.

The school had a democratic and chivalrous character. Unlike women, male students were required to work a certain amount; to wait on themselves, draw their own water, and tend their own fires. The academic atmosphere was not stifling: one student nearly convinced Addison Clark to believe in the theory of evolution. Years later, Clark and his wife laughed long and loud when recalling the debate. Some professors were hardly any older than their students. One professor, Ben Parks, came promptly when told a student named Miss Wade wished to speak to him at study hall. There he found a gleeful crowd of students waiting to see him blush, but no Miss Wade. Parks and Wade later married.

The students housed ad hoc among locals. They came from Texas primarily, mostly from nearby counties, although by 1890 the students hailed from eighty-two counties and six other states. Add Ran College built a girls' dorm in 1883, and by 1888 several "cottages" were erected on the grounds to house students.

Thorp Spring treated the fledgling college well enough to ward off advances from Fort Worth, which wanted the school back. Five years after the Panic of '73 the economy was still depressed, and Mr. Thorp agreed to cancel the Clarks' promissory notes, which the teachers could not pay. In return, they gave Thorp ownership of the building that housed the school, and for a time the school paid rent.

Although the prestige of the school grew, it continued to face financial struggles, and in September of 1889 the Clarks turned over ownership of the school to the Christian Churches of Texas. The administration remained with the family, but the board of trustees now came from the Church, which secured a new charter from the state in October, changing the name of the school to "Add Ran Christian College." The school added its first graduate degree, a Masters of Arts, in 1891.

Four years later, Add Ran would move again, farther south to Waco, in the heart of Texas cotton country. Waco had attracted immigration from Europe and the war-torn South, and by 1889 it had a population exceeding fourteen thousand. It began predominantly as a Methodist town, the Methodists having formed Waco's first church in 1851. The Baptist Mission Board, which at first did not consider Waco promising enough to send a missionary, reversed course and supported a missionary beginning in 1851. That year, Judge Baylor preached the first Baptist sermon in the town, renting the church from the Methodists; the Baptists would have their own building by 1857. The two denominations cooperated to form a boys' high school called Trinity College. The Methodists looked out for

Add Ran faculty, Thorp Spring, 1890.

their girls, too, and founded the Methodist Female College. The curriculum focused on music recitals and elocution, and the administrators punished inappropriate contact between the sexes by forcing miscreants to drink castor oil.

Trinity College rebranded as Waco University in 1861, and in 1866 the Baptist General Association of Texas decided to move its fledgling institution, Baylor University, to Waco and consolidate it with Waco University. With the arrival of Baylor in 1866, Waco became more Baptist than Methodist. Despite the competition the Methodist Female College prospered for a few years, eventually changing its name to Waco Female College. But while Baylor University flourished, Waco Female College floundered, and its building was seized by a creditor in 1890.

The Christian Church was late to the scene in Waco, but by late 1895 a collection of Wacoans, headed by the Waco Christian Church and Waco Commercial Club, approached Add Ran Christian College. They offered to buy the former Waco Female College building and give it to Add Ran if Add Ran would move to Waco. The College agreed—over Addison Clark's objections—and near Christmas Day 1895, the professors and students, including Addison Clark, traveled to Waco together and formed a procession down the street from the Waco train station to a formal welcoming ceremony at the First Baptist Church, where Baylor University's president gave one of the welcoming speeches.

EARLY FOOTBALL

The sport of football began to establish itself in Texas in the 1890s. Mark F. Bernstein described American sport following the Civil War:

> American sport at the end of the Civil War was heavily stratified
> by class. The wealthy followed horse racing and cricket, while
> boxing and later baseball appealed more to a working-class au-
> dience. [Joseph] Pulitzer had initially scorned football as a game
> for rich college boys, but by the early 1890s had come to appre-
> ciate its broader appeal. Football, especially at the prominent
> Ivy colleges, played to both highbrow and lowbrow audiences.[4]

Football developed out of a version of English Rugby—Rugby being the name of a school—and appeared at undergraduate rushes at Yale about the time white settlers began settling along the Brazos and Trinity Rivers in Central and North Texas. The games were violent, as described by one witness of early football strategy: "The main object of this game was the elimination of the opponent by constantly kicking him on the shins until he was forced to retire from the game."[5] Faculties routinely banned football games, but the sport's appeal outran the academics' opposition.

In 1874, the Harvard team played the McGill University team in Montreal using traditional rugby rules, which allowed players to run with the ball, making movement down the field considerably easier. The Americans discovered that they liked the Canadian rules very much, so the Crimson brought their enthusiasm for rugby-style football back to the States and convinced Yale (despite beating them handily) to adopt the new rules. Walter Camp, a Yale man, became obsessed with the new version of the sport, which by 1876 was still a simple series of coordinated headlong rushes (called "fairs") into an equally headlong defensive pile called "scrummages." That year student representatives from Harvard, Yale, Princeton, and the University of Pennsylvania met in Springfield, Massachusetts, to settle on some common rules for the game. They adopted the Canadian rules for running with the ball and tackling—above the waist only.

Four years later, representatives from Yale, Rutgers, Princeton, and Columbia met to form the first intercollegiate association in the nation and to revise rules for the game yet again. They adopted Camp's proposal that changed the rugby-style scrum to a cleaner line of scrimmage, with the ball being put in play by a player's foot into the hands of a player in a newly-created position—the "quarter-back"—instead of being tossed into a scrum by the referee. Creating the line of scrimmage separated American football from rugby. For fostering this change, and for nurturing football in its early years, Walter Camp is considered the father of football. Camp

"A thud of bodies," from the *Horned Frog* (yearbook) of 1907.

started publishing an annual guide to football in the mid–1880s, and began choosing an all-American team every year starting in 1888, focusing first on Ivy League players but soon traveling the country to observe notable players elsewhere.

Playing with a line of scrimmage but without a minimum yardage requirement for downs created perverse incentives. These incentives ruined a championship game between Yale and Princeton in 1881. Both teams were aiming for a tie, because each considered itself the defending champion. Princeton held the ball for the entire first half, simply moving backwards on each snap, repeatedly netting touchbacks. Yale repeated the feat in the second half. This misfire of the rules prompted a third rules convention in 1882, where the Canadian system of downs was adopted for the American game. Teams now had to move the ball forward five yards in three downs.

Scoring was imprecise until 1882, when numerical values were assigned to various kinds of plays: five points for field goals, four for touchdowns, and two for kicks after touchdowns.

Blocking for the ball carrier (then called "interference") became legal in 1888, as did tackling below the waist. These changes encouraged the closely bunched formations in midfield that still characterized early football. Because linemen were not required to play at the line of scrimmage, blocking for the ball carrier could be taken to extremes with wedge plays. For the infamous "Flying Wedge" play, the center would begin alone at the line of scrimmage, snapping the ball back ten or twenty yards to the rest of his team, which was bunched together and already running towards the defense. The play must have been terrifying; occasionally it was lethal. The Flying Wedge was specifically outlawed in 1894 with the restriction that only two players could be in motion in the backfield before the snap. It lived on, however, in subtle variations called "guards back," "tackles back," and "mass on tackle" plays. In these "mass plays," linemen would line up in the backfield and then attempt to pull or push the ball carrier through the defensive line.

In the 1880s, conferences of colleges emerged to combat the expense and violence of the game, and also to prevent the use of "tramp" athletes who would play on the team—sometimes just for the big Thanksgiving game—but not attend class or even enroll in school. The 1880s also saw football begin to spread westward as students who saw or played the game at Ivy League schools went to schools in other parts of the country. The newer teams usually played without a coach and with little more guidance than Walter Camp's *Annual Guide*.

Most prominent in this westward drift was Amos Alonzo Stagg, an all-American at Yale, who was recruited by the founder of the University of Chicago in 1892 to attend the university, establish the athletic department, and forge a football team. (About a decade later A. C. Easley brought a rulebook to Add Ran from Alonzo Stagg; it was probably a recent edition of Camp's *Annual Guide*.) In 1890 there was enough student interest in the sport in the West for the formation of the Western Intercollegiate Football Association.

FOOTBALL COMES TO TEXAS

By the 1890s, football reached Texas. City teams appeared first: Dallas and Fort Worth both had teams that played in 1891 before several hundred spectators. Fort Worth's first team, called the "Heavyweights," began play in 1890. Austin College and Texas A&M each organized football teams, only to disband them by 1895 after only two "seasons" of intercollegiate play. Only the University of Texas's team, which played as early as 1891, managed a continuous existence into the twentieth century. Fort Worth University and Polytechnic University both were playing intramural contests in 1892, but they were not playing against each other.

It is not known whether any students from the Add Ran Christian College traveled to Dallas from Thorp Spring in November of 1893 to witness the game between the heralded Dallas Foot Ball Club and a student team from the University of Texas—or perhaps to witness a bicyclist's attempts to break three cycling records during halftime. The team at the University of Texas had agreed to play the Dallas Foot Ball Club in 1892, but backed out of the agreement by telegram the day before the game, giving the excuse that the team couldn't sacrifice its preparations for its college field day. The UT team agreed again to play the Dallas team in

8

1893 for a guarantee of $200. Its ball burst in one practice scrimmage for the contest, and the players had to wait while a student bicycled into town to buy another one.

The match was held on November 11, 1893, in front of about two thousand onlookers. The sport that the spectators came to watch only resembled modern football. The largest player on either team weighed 210 pounds. During halftime, while the competitive cyclist tried to break the records, the referee quit because the Dallas team complained so much. A spectator who was a member of the Fort Worth club filled in as referee for the second half. The students prevailed, handing the Dallas team its first-ever loss.

The sport was already positioning itself as the primary identifier of colleges. The Princeton-Yale game on Thanksgiving of 1893 was as big a spectacle of sport and school pride as any game in our day. By 1902, TCU's *Skiff* could proclaim, "Football to a large extent is the criterion by which one institution measures another. To lose means discredit. To win means to command the respect not only of other schools but outsiders also."[6]

Even though rapid maturation and major rule changes from 1906 to 1912 were yet to come, a humorous 1904 essay in the *Skiff* already carries the familiar flavor of the game. It depicts a frustrated fan trying to explain the sport to his date:

> "O, no, no, no, no, no; you haven't got it at all. The fullback is sometimes built that way, but the term is not used to describe figure. They call him the fullback to distinguish his position from that of the halfbacks."
>
> "Oh!" she exclaimed. "In that case I should [think] they would call him the whole back. That would sound better, don't you think? But never mind: I suppose I must not be too critical about terms when there is so much that I want to learn. It's a combination game, isn't it?"
>
> "Combination of what?" he asked.
>
> "Why, of football and handball, of course."
>
> "O, no, no, no, no, no, no," he said, wearily.
>
> "Then why do they take the ball in their hands?" she demanded.
>
> "To carry it," he exclaimed.
>
> "But, if it's football," she urged, "I should think they would have to carry it with their feet. How far do they have to carry it?"
>
> "As far as they can. You see, the distance is marked by lines."
>
> "O, yes; now I understand!" she cried, delightedly.

"I've heard you talk of five-yard lines and ten-yard lines and all that, and of course that's the way you score. Five yards count five, and so on. I've often wondered why there were such big scores in football."

There were many people laughing by this time, but the young man could only say, wearily, "O, no, no, no, no, no; you don't get it at all."

"It's awfully complicated, don't you think?" she sighed, "but I'll get it all right after a while. I'm sure I'm beginning to understand it. Now, which of those long white lines is the rush line?

"I told you once," he replied, "that those were the five-yard lines. The rush line is composed of players."

"How foolish of me," she said. "I ought to have remembered that. Now, where is the left tackle?"

The young man pointed to the player in that position.

"Oh!" she exclaimed, disappointed. "I thought tackle was rigging, or rope, or something like fishing tackle, you know. . . ."

"Mabel," said the youth, at last, "Don't ask me anything more about football."[7]

VOLUNTEER COACHES, GREEN PLAYERS

College football in the small colleges of Texas retained the trappings of an intramural sport for many years. Professors doubled as coaches. Schools and coaches did not know which players would be on the team until they showed up—already enrolled—for the first practices. In 1902, TCU held its first practices of the season as much to teach the boys how to play the game as to sort out a depth chart or develop technique. The coach did not choose a first team from his players until one day prior to the opening game. The University of Texas, by contrast, not only had a coach, but fielded four teams drawn from fifty players.

However familiar to its fans at the turn of the twentieth century, football was still quite unlike the modern game. It was almost exclusively a school sport, perhaps like lacrosse is in America today. Teams did not have full-time professional coaches until the University of Texas hired the first in the state in 1899. The season did not begin until October. Teams would practice their signals before each game, and games lasted up to seventy minutes. Time-outs were not added until 1905, and the halves were not split into quarters until 1909. The quarterback was prevented from running with the ball; he was not allowed that privilege for a decade.

There were many fewer officials on the field at games; only one is reported at the University of Texas versus Dallas game. After the famous

"Spectators," from the *Horned Frog,* 1906.

1906 rule changes, most games had only two: a referee and an umpire. Apparently, teams were penalized for playing offsides, or interfering with catching a punt, but penalty yardage did not increase the distance required to convert; it merely moved possession farther away from the opponent's goal without changing the down or the distance required for a first down.

The teams each played eleven men at a time, down from as many as fifteen in earlier years, but no one wore numbers or lined up wide, or thought of himself as a receiver. The forward pass was still illegal; the "flying wedge" legal. The positions were not all the same as in the modern sport. Offenses had seven linemen: two "ends" outside of the traditional tackles, guards, and center as in the modern sport. The "ends" were something like modern blocking tight ends in a rush-based offense—they were blockers. When the forward pass became legal, the ends ran downfield to catch them.

A quartet of players stood behind the line as if at the four points of a diamond—a quarterback, a left and a right halfback, and a fullback. Any one of the players except the quarterback was as likely as others to carry the ball. Whoever was toting the rock could not cross the line of scrimmage in the middle of the field, but rather had to move at least five yards off of center before crossing the line. For variation—and trickery—players in the backfield would pitch the ball to each other, hoping to catch a defense overcommitting. Punting was a much larger part of the game than it is today. Teams punted on any down, taking satisfaction in moving the opponent far away from the goal line. Often the quarterback was the team's best punter. There was no huddling between plays. Rather, the quarterback or another signal-calling player would bark out plays at the line, something like the modern no-huddle offense.

The player with the ball likely pursued one of two types of plays: "line bucks," or "end runs." Line bucking was the typical play, and gave rise to the cliché "three yards and a cloud of dust." The *Skiff* described it this way: "The man with the ball must buck into the opposing line and then fall his full length ahead . . . [for gains of] two yards each. . . . [T]his battering ram method is much more certain of results than a run around the end." The *Skiff* then quoted a football expert's description:

> The modern theory is one of pure momentum and nothing else. Momentum is the product of weight multiplied by speed, e.g. a player weighing two hundred pounds moving at ten feet per second represents a momentum of two thousand at the point of impact. A combination of two, three, or four players of same weight and speed raises this figure to four thousand, six thousand, or eight thousand. The theory is to concentrate this momentum upon a point whose powers of resistance must necessarily be less; in other words, the stronger attack the weaker. The entire variation in the game is due merely to the attempt to find the weak spot in the opposing line. Plays are directed repeatedly against one player for the express purpose of weakening him, and thereby creating a weaker spot.[8]

Reporters—who were warming to football very quickly—had never been housed in a press box. What the press did write about games was just beginning to appear on the front pages of newspapers, or in sports sections. Joseph Pulitzer pioneered the sports page in his *New York World*, which soon was mimicked across the country. It wasn't until 1895 that marquee games in the Ivy League—which was still by far the most important football league of the day—got banner headlines on the front pages of notable newspapers.

The student body was expected to follow the Ivy League example and attend each of their team's practices. TCU, SMU, and Baylor's papers were all convinced this commitment from the students would prompt better performance from the faithful players—and encourage the slackers to show up. The *Skiff* urged in 1902, "If the ladies would grace the grandstand with their presence each afternoon and make the air ring with their shouts, more of the boys would come out to practice. They would work harder."[9] Baylor's coach was less obliging, scolding his school's students in 1904, "If you wish Baylor to win, it is necessary that you aid us, not only by united cheering but also by daily encouraging the players at practice, and by aid-ing them to observe the rules of training."[10] SMU's school paper's editors wrote in 1918, "It is not enough that we yell at pep meetings; we must show the men that we are interested in their practice hours by coming out and rooting on the sidelines every afternoon."[11]

THE BOYS FROM THE HEIGHTS

One 1895 Add Ran College alum "often enthused over his own football experiences [in Thorp Spring] before his graduation."[12] Those experiences would have been exclusively intramural. Add Ran did not have any intercollegiate sports yet, but the baseball and football games between students were organized well enough to warrant attention in the *Collegian*, the school paper published in Thorp Spring before Add Ran moved to Waco. But football and baseball took a backseat to military drill, which was the most popular organized extracurricular activity for students at Add Ran, much as it was in colleges all across the old South. Two companies were formed at Add Ran College in 1895.

An anti-sports attitude in the administration at Add Ran, beginning with Addison Clark himself, posed a bigger obstacle to football than the popularity of military drill. Clark, like most older men of his generation, had little use or tolerance for sports. He preferred that the virtues of strength and endurance be acquired by work, not by frivolity. He made an exception to his somber lifestyle for hiking, and would often lead the boys on hikes up to twenty miles across the country.

An 1876-77 school catalog described the near-Puritan expectation for student culture in that early day. The students were . . .

> . . . to have neither the time nor the desire for miscella-
> neous gallantry, or letter writing. . . . That they attend
> no exhibition of immoral tendency; no race course, the-
> ater, circus, billiard saloon, bar-room, or tippling house.
> . . . That they abstain from profanity, the desecration of
> the Lord's Day, all kinds of gaming for a reward or prize of
> any kind, and from card playing even for amusement.
> . . . That they attend public worship every Lord's Day.[13]

Alcohol consumption and tobacco use were likewise prohibited, as was leaving the college without permission. Uniforms, although not required until 1882, were wool and gray (with checked gingham aprons for the girls). Jewelry and hairdos with bangs were forbidden. The school administrators checked on the students in their rooms nightly, and boasted of the orderliness they observed (or enforced).

Addison "Little Addie" Clark Jr., 1897 or 1898.

The college prohibited dating with appalling zeal. One coed was reprimanded for walking across campus with a male student—her brother!—because it gave the appearance of evil. Shortly before commencement in 1892, a male student was found to have walked his fiancée from town to her house, and was immediately and publicly expelled. Other students petitioned Addison Clark to reinstate the student, saying that they all had stolen privileges at one time or another during their years at school. Clark responded by expelling all of them, too, prompting the school's first admissions crisis. Mrs. Jarvis, who was Add Ran's headmistress of housing for women, interceded on behalf of the expelled students, and Clark relented—and began the practice of hosting monthly socials for the students. One Add Ran alum recalled talking a girl to sleep at one of the regular soirees the school held during its Thorp Spring days.

Clark eventually proved flexible regarding sports on campus, as well. Clark's son, "Little Addie," returned from studies at the University of Michigan in 1896 with an abiding enthusiasm for football. After Addie hired on at Add Ran to teach, his father Addison warmed to the game—or to his son's enthusiasm for it—and ceased opposing it on campus. This remarkable turnaround is the first significant debt that TCU football fans owe to Midwestern football.

The second debt to the Midwest came in the person of Aaron C. Easley, one of six children of William and Phoebe Easley, who had originally come to Texas in 1871 and staked a claim near the Red River. In 1882, William brought Aaron and his younger brother one hundred miles by

Main building, Waco campus, 1897.

wagon to Add Ran's campus. "I know you are going to make good," said his father, "and we are going to do our best to bring you back (home) every year 'til you graduate, and then we are counting on you to help us put the other children through college."[11] (A. C. fulfilled that responsibility; his sister Julia Easley Robertson, an 1896 graduate, was on the committee that recommended purple and white as school colors.)

William set out with the wagon once again to bring A. C. home from school after his first year. Forty miles from Thorp Spring, he succumbed to pneumonia, and died one day before his son was able to reach him. The saddened student borrowed a horse for the journey home. "I shall never forget the feeling of responsibility that swept over me as I rode up to the house and Mother and my brothers and sisters ran out to meet me. It looked like my chance for an education was gone."[14]

A. C.'s younger brothers were old enough to tend the farm by 1885, and A. C. returned to Add Ran, taking the same job he had before: doing chores at the residents' homes and sweeping and making fires in the school building. A. C. married an Add Ran student and joined the faculty after graduating. Family lore credits Easley for first suggesting to the Christian Church that it purchase Add Ran.

Easley went to the Midwest in the summer of 1896 to study at the University of Chicago, which had been established just five years earlier. While in Chicago, he became a fan of the new sport from the east. He met Alonzo Stagg and obtained a new football rulebook from him. He returned to Waco in the fall and joined Little Addie in organizing a football game among the students on Thanksgiving Day, 1896. Different colored stockings sufficed for uniforms: one team wore brown, the other black. They played three more games after Thanksgiving, beating Toby's Business College, losing to Houston's Heavyweights 22-0 on December 19, and then tying Houston's Heavyweights in the rematch sometime later that month. The "season" was a draw, as the team finished with a 1-1-1 record.

An athletic association was formed that leased a field on the southwest corner of the Waco campus early in January 1897. Addison Clark had become so much a supporter of football, and athletics in general, that he argued in favor of intercollegiate play in other Texas cities before a skeptical board of trustees early that year. The board grudgingly added the "requirement of athletic exercises as a part of University courses," but refused to allow the football team to play at College Station, Austin, or Houston—even though Clark had already accepted invitations to play from A&M, UT, and a Houston team. Discouraged, but not disbanded, the school's football enthusiasts pressed forward, reorganizing the athletic association in September, and appointing as manager W. O. Stephens, who filled most of the functions of a modern athletic director and equipment manager. Stephens raised enough money to hire a coach, Joe Y. Field, who arrived on the first of October.[15]

Field coached Add Ran's first memorable team, called sometimes the "boys from the Heights" of north Waco. No Horned Frogs would match them for a decade. Years later, M. R. Sharp would reminisce about how there were "only about thirty boys in school—yet they had a winning football club."[16] The lineup was left end Frank Pruett, left tackle Guy Green, left guard W. G. Carnahan, center Sam Rutledge (in 1903 still called TCU's best center to date), right guard (and future athletic director) C. I. Alexander, right tackle R. Earle Sparks, right end Claude McClellan, (who was also team captain), quarterback C. W. Herring, left halfback M. R. Sharp, right halfback Jim V. McClintic, and fullback Jeff R. Sypert. S. S. Glasscock, R. Holt, G. A. Foote, and H. E. Field played backup.

Add Ran's athletic association won permission from the board of trustees to travel out of Waco for games two weeks before the opener against a team in Dallas that was unaffiliated with any college. Add Ran won 6-0. Traveling apparently suited the Horned Frogs, for they were one of the first college teams ever to score on the University of Texas. The Wacoans played the Austinites "to a standstill," losing 16–10 (one account lists the score 18-10).[17] Texas A&M and Fort Worth University, on the other hand, were no match for the upstarts from north Waco, losing 30-6 and 32-0, respectively.[18]

Perhaps Coach Field's players' success stemmed from their training regimen, laid down by the coach: "1. Abstain from all intoxicants, also coffee and tobacco. 2. Go to bed at ten. 3. Eat no sweets or pastry. 4. Indulge

The Boys from the Heights: Add Ran football team, 1897.

in no kinds of dissipation."[19] Or perhaps the success came from the team's new mascot, the horned frog, a common lizard in Central Texas before fire ants migrated to Texas in the 1950s and drove the horned frog away. It could have been stimulated by the school's new colors, purple and white, chosen by representative coeds from both of Add Ran's literary societies. (The team wore blue on its uniforms, however, until 1912.)

Add Ran's 3-1-0 record in 1897 would be its best mark for the following decade, which was darkened first by strangling opposition from the administration, and then by a stretch of losses so demoralizing that the school nearly quit the sport altogether. It is doubtful that the school actually awarded letters at the end of the 1897 season, but today TCU recognizes sixteen letter winners from that year—the entire team.

Football at Add Ran began amid substantial headwinds from the trustees and the Christian Church about whether or not football was an appropriate exercise for its students. Winning in 1897 did nothing to calm the storm of football doubters and non-supporters at Add Ran. The divinity students apparently did not share their elders' doubts about vigorous exercise and team sports, however. Several students studying divinity joined the team, including Colby D. Hall, giving it an evangelical flavor it retained for some years. Hall was the university pastor in later years, and wrote the only substantial book on TCU's early history that has survived into the twenty-first century.

Charles Edwin Bull (1898 photo) always packed his pistol when away from home.

James Morrison took over the coaching duties for the '98 season. Morrison was most likely a professor already on campus who took no extra pay for his work as coach. Returning fullback Jeff Sypert was the new captain, elected at the end of the 1897 season by his teammates.

The team had enough support from the administration to warrant meals supplied by the school after practice, but not so much as to get permission to travel away from Waco. In September the board of trustees again voted on the matter of inter-city travel for athletics—this time voting it down. Addison Clark may have changed with the times, but the Christian Church had not. The sentiment was not unique to the older generation of the Disciples of Christ Church. Baylor's longtime president, Rufus Burleson, flatly refused to allow Baylor students to play football; the Bears didn't field a team until Burleson retired to *emeritus* status in 1899.

The team traveled nonetheless, including to Midland on Thanksgiving, playing in the snow. The rough and tumble match so angered an attending wealthy cattleman that he offered one of the trustees two thousand dollars if Add Ran would eschew football entirely.

Add Ran played miserably in 1898, scoring only on hapless Toby's Business College (beating them 41-0). Add Ran lost to the University of Texas twice and Texas A&M once, and settled for a scoreless tie with the Fort Worth University Packers. The win over Toby's Business College was Add Ran's last victory over a college team for six years. Only two letter winners from the '97 team garnered second letters in '98 (again, probably only awarded in media guides printed decades later).

Perhaps chastened by the team's dismal showing on the field, Addison Clark promised the trustees that his college's players would not travel outside of Waco again. All was not lost that year, however. Halfback Jim V. McClintic's father, G. V. McClintic, was a trustee of the college, and

> had all but forbidden his son Jim, one of the stars, to play the rough game. The father came to a game down in the old Padgitt's Park in Waco, against the University of Texas. He sat doggedly on the topmost seat in the grandstand, grimly determined not to enjoy the rough stuff. As the game progressed, the father slipped down a row or two, then another and another, until long before the second half, he was on the front row yelling like a Comanche. Jim was knocked cold that day and didn't recover until an hour after the game was finished, but the father was so soundly converted that this did not faze him. It was football that went to glory; Jim survived and went to Congress (serving the Seventh District, Oklahoma, for two decades beginning in 1915).[20]

The 1898 season also gives Frog fans the colorful story of Charles Edwin Bull—newly enrolled that fall and having never heard of the game of football. Jim McClintic convinced him to try it out, and upon being tackled the first time, by G. A. Foote, Bull said, "To hell with this kind of a game—I'm through with this foolishness," and then he quit. But McClintic managed to talk him back onto the team, and before long Bull was one of the starting guards on the line. In one of the games at Austin that season, McClintic and Bull roomed together, and McClintic was shocked to see Bull put a pistol under his belt while dressing for the game. To McClintic's surprised query came Bull's famous reply, "I always wear my pistol when away from home and among strangers," adding that he'd never lost it in any tussle he'd ever had. McClintic talked him out of wearing the gun to the game.[21]

The Church's and board's opposition to football grew increasingly ef-

Add Ran football team, 1899. The "pendants" hanging from several players' necks are nose guards.

fective the next year, in 1899. That year they enforced their prohibition on travel away from Waco, meaning Add Ran had only Baylor University for an opponent that season. Why the team did not play Toby's Business College that year (Toby's played Baylor twice) is a mystery now lost to history. Baylor fielded its first team that year, and held the more experienced Frogs to a scoreless tie. Jim V. McClintic was team captain in 1899, but he does not appear on the modern list of lettermen.

The board of trustees' opposition to football reached its zenith in 1900. Add Ran's team played no games that year. C. I. Alexander was the team captain, as much as he had a team to be captain of at all, and is the first Horned Frog to be considered a three-year letterman. Alexander is the only player listed on the letterman roster for 1900. The single-name list is a mute witness to the very real possibility that football at Add Ran might have died with the new century—and TCU football might never have existed at all.

1901

The year without a football season must have dampened the school's morale. The board of trustees, softened by the addition of a couple of new members, retreated in their campaign against football in 1901. The board paid for new uniforms for the team, and even allowed it to play out of town.

Playing the games, however, did not dispel the clouds that darkened the program after its winning campaign of '97. No period in the history of TCU football—not even the years following the walking death penalty in the mid-1980s—was as miserable as the coachless years 1899 through 1904. What the administration accomplished for a year by fiat—no football at Add Ran—the team itself nearly accomplished by consistently losing. Add Ran learned that winning on the football field requires first winning in the administration. It would forget that lesson before the century was out.

The school's modern media guides show no coaches for 1899 through 1901, and none for 1903. H. E. Hildebrand (1902) and C. E. Cronk (1904) are each listed as coaches during this period, but contemporary records indicate the team did not get two seasons' worth of coaching in those years. The name C. E. Cronk does not show up in the *Skiff*'s pages during 1904; from early in the season the student paper reported the coach to be a Professor Hamner. The discrepancy hardly mattered. Within a few weeks it appeared the team was again coachless, whoever carried the title in September.

As is often true of bad football teams, the coachless TCU football teams had some excellent players who would have stood out on any team. Two such players made names for themselves on Add Ran's team beginning in 1901. Lineman A. J. "The Heavenly" Muse began his football career that season, and fullback Wade Shumate returned to the gridiron as captain of the team, having already lettered one year in 1899.

The 1901 season began with a win over Taylor High School, which Add Ran followed with a tie against the Trinity Tigers, a Presbyterian college in Waxahachie. The game would not have been scoreless had TCU not fumbled away multiple scoring opportunities deep in Trinity's territory. These performances were good enough, however, to win praise from Baylor University's student newspaper, the *Lariat*.

The season concluded with two games against Baylor. The first was a fiasco, as both teams had the dropsies and fumbled often. Baylor's superior blocking, however, freed its backfield to make long end runs. Add Ran rarely converted, and never got within thirty yards of a score, although Shumate ran for a few good gains. Baylor sent in subs for much of the second half. The *Lariat* rebuked both teams, saying, "neither team played foot ball; Add Ran because they did not know how; Baylor because they were not forced to."[22] The final score was 36-0. Add Ran suffered even greater humiliation in the second game, losing to Baylor 42-0. Since the Frogs had managed to beat only a high school team, Add Ran's administration seriously considered dropping football altogether.

1902

Add Ran Christian College at last became Texas Christian University in 1902—the same year that the venerable *Skiff* began publication, replacing the old (and now lost) *Collegian*. The school sent delegates to the meeting of Texas's nascent athletics conference, the Texas Intercollegiate Athletics Association (TIAA), which began to expand its jurisdiction beyond track and field. TCU also hired a coach, its first since 1898, and only the third in its history. Whoever the hire—H. E. Hildebrand or Professor Hamner—the coach did not last more than a couple weeks into the season.

TCU had lined up six games with three opponents. The team would meet Baylor's team three times, Trinity's Tigers twice, including the opener, and A&M's Farmers once. Lineman A. J. Muse returned with halfback Wade Shumate, but otherwise the team was largely new. By the opener, a new student named Homer Rowe had moved from the line to the backfield. Clad in TCU's blue sweater, and sporting fiery red hair against pale white skin, he garnered the nicknames "Old Glory" and "Star-Spangled." In practice before the season, the first team did not play the second team—at least not very much—and did not tackle low enough.

The '02 season opened on a Monday at West End Park against Trinity's experienced team from Waxahachie. Baylor's coach was the umpire; one representative each from Trinity and TCU were referees called "linemen." In later years it would be common for a coach from one of the teams to be a timekeeper. Trinity whipped TCU with unfamiliar moves and aggressive line play. The squad from Waxahachie, led by players named Guyer and Steel, made repeated gains of ten and fifteen yards, confusing the Wacoans with hurdles, double passes, and quarterback kicks. By the end the crowd, which the *Lariat* called "quite light," was quiet, and the score was 28-0, Trinity.

The first meeting of TCU and Baylor in 1902 was held at Baylor's field and ended in a fumble-ridden scoreless tie. Baylor played without three of its best players—Lester, Wicker, and Vanham. TCU drove the ball repeatedly and well, but fumbled away possession multiple times near Baylor's goal. The *Lariat* cited a lack of teamwork as the cause of TCU's inability to score, but credited TCU's captain Shumate as "easily the star of the TCU team and would show up well in any Texas team."[23]

After a rainy bye week for TCU, Texas A&M came to Waco to meet the Horned Frogs for the first time in four years. The Farmers thoroughly impressed the Wacoans with their 22-0 knockout. The *Skiff* wrote, "The A&M team showed up well. They have weight, training, and science of the game. . . . The team is an honor to their school and the state. It is the best team that has been seen in Waco for many days and promises to be the best in the South before the season closes."[24] The Farmers from College

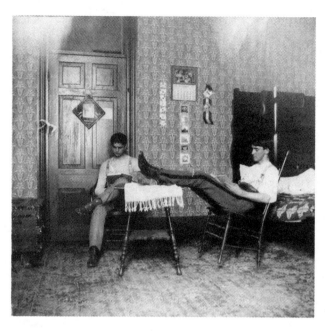
Fullback Wade Shumate (right) relaxes in the dorm, about 1902.

Station won the state championship, informal as it was, that season.

Rain muddied the practice fields so regularly that TCU could practice only once or twice a week. TCU went to its second game with Baylor in '02 without both of its starting ends, and suffered for it on offense. Aside from one series late in the game, when A. J. Muse gained thirty yards around left end, TCU was punchless with the ball. It converted only one possession. Without the ball, however, the team slowly stiffened, and by the second half was playing splendid defense. TCU intercepted a Baylor pitch, and pushed Baylor backwards after they had driven inside TCU's one-yard line. Baylor won 6-0. After listing a few excuses, the *Skiff* announced that it could make no excuses, "Baylor just got down and out played us, that's all. Nine 'rahs for the boys that beat us."[25]

TCU made its first road trip of the season—likely its first road trip in five years—to play the Trinity Tigers at Waxahachie, leaving by train at 5:00 a.m. Thanksgiving Day, and kicking off after 4:00 p.m. The winless Frogs put up a fight in the first half, Shumate and Muse tallying multiple stops behind Trinity's line, "to the surprise and admiration of the [mostly local] spectators." When not behind the line on one play, Muse knocked his counterpart tackle across the line "sky west and crooked."[26] Trinity scored first, and only escaped being scored on when the referee, after TCU drew a fifteen-yard penalty, mistakenly added fifteen yards to the distance TCU was required to gain to convert. TCU's drive ended on the next play, and the Horned Frogs did not threaten to score again. Trinity used trick plays—which the *Skiff* called famous, but did not describe for posterity— and scored twice more before the game was called for darkness.

TCU hosted Baylor for the season finale, in a drizzle.[27] Baylor scored four times before TCU finally answered, when Homer Rowe recovered a fumble near midfield and carried it fifty-five yards for a touchdown— only to have the play called back for an offsides penalty. By this time, the Horned Frogs' series with Baylor—two or three games per season—had coalesced into a rivalry. It was not yet bitter, though. Baylor thought of TCU as its little brother, and although neither school had a win to its name in October, the sentiment among the Baptists was that however bad the season might be, at least Baylor would be able to beat TCU. Baylor fans cheered both teams in the third match in 1902, and after Baylor thoroughly drubbed the Horned Frogs in 1903, the *Lariat* went out of its way to compliment the Frogs' effort.

The hapless Frogs ended the year winless, 0-5-1, and worse, scoreless for the entire season. The team reelected Wade Shumate as captain, and hoped for the best. More doldrums awaited.

1903

Playing again without a coach in 1903—and also without a trainer—the team again lacked discipline and leadership. Some good players stayed away from the game or participated intermittently. Junior Wade Shumate was not listed as team captain when the season got underway in October. End Clovis Moore carried the title by the season opener. Moore was a veteran, having played in Add Ran's only game in 1899 and at tackle in 1902. Tackle A. J. Muse—now in his third year—and sophomore Charles Ashmore led the team.

TCU had never really intimidated Baylor, and continued that dismal trend in 1903, one of the Horned Frogs' most miserable seasons. In the season opener against Baylor, TCU never forced their opponents to punt—a dubious distinction in an era when punting was a primary weapon. The game was well attended, considering the street cars were not running and that there was a "monkey show" in town competing for an audience. The Frogs' quarterback Napoleon Grissom, who was small in stature, was said to have resembled a mosquito on an elephant when he was dragged for several yards after tackling a much bigger Baylor player.

The *Lariat* wrote that Baylor won "of course. We expected that. . . ." But the Baylor paper complimented the crosstown rivals, continuing:

A. Jack "The Heavenly" Muse, captain of the 1904 team. The 1905 yearbook declared that "as a general and as a ground gainer [he] had no equal."

At all stages of the game we 'knew they were over there,' and such a determined stand did they make to prevent the first touchdown, that it seemed like two mighty mountains had moved against each other, each struggling for supremacy, so unmoved was each line, until such an irresistible surge was made, such as only Baylor's magnificent team can make, that it sent Milton and the ball through the opponents' line and beyond the goal.[28]

The *Lariat*'s compliments did not extend to TCU's repeated time-outs for broken shoestrings, which the Baylor fans thought feigned.

TCU's first match with Texas A&M was what is called today a "trap game" for A&M. The Farmers were again considered among the state's best in '03. Many of TCU's players switched to different positions—Muse from left to right tackle, Woods from right to left tackle, Napoleon Grissom from quarter- to halfback. Ends C. Smith and Clovis Moore started. Fred Obenchain, Charles Ashmore, and Kelner played as subs. The merry-go-round of position switches at TCU worked wonders. TCU made remarkable gains in the game's first half hour, scoring the only touchdown before halftime, and keeping the Aggies on their own end of the field for the first half.

Texas A&M's star guard, Benjamin, came in at the half and turned the tide, but not before TCU threatened another touchdown before fumbling the ball at the A&M fifteen-yard line. Homer Rowe had some long carries in the game, but took a pounding for them. A&M called TCU's tackles Muse and Wood the best they'd played against. TCU lost, but only 22–6. The *Skiff* claimed that the game at College Station was "one of the fiercest for football honors ever fought on a Southern gridiron."[29]

Playing A&M so closely raised expectations in Waco about the home team. Trinity promptly dashed those expectations. TCU fielded almost the same lineup in Waxahachie as in College Station, but Trinity was one of the best in the state and clobbered the Frogs 30–0. Quarterback Homer Rowe played through his injuries. Despite its comfortable-looking win, Trinity claimed the following week to be so hobbled by injuries and parental objections that it could not play Baylor, TCU, or anybody else the rest of that season.

When Trinity backed out of its scheduled return game, it created an empty week for the Frogs that TCU filled with a trip to Daniel Baker College in Brownwood. What TCU did not fill, however, was the train car to Brownwood. Four Horned Frog starters did not make the trip, and the team returned home losers, 10–5.

The last match with Baylor in '03 was held on a cool Thanksgiving Day. The closest either team came to scoring in the first half was a blocked Baylor field goal attempt. Homer Rowe racked up yards on end-arounds—in some plays 20 at a time—behind A. J. Muse's aggressive blocking. TCU made memorable defensive stands on its three- and one-yard lines in the second half, getting the ball back on downs each time. The boys from the Heights did not get a win for their stupendous defensive effort, because they fumbled the ball away near their goal and could not keep Baylor out of their goal a third time. Baylor missed the point after, but won the game 5–0.

A&M came to north Waco for the season finale, and again failed to beat TCU as badly as expected. The Farmers did score once each half, and sustained long drives of many short bucks, most for just a handful of yards. The 11–0 loss for TCU made a second winless, untied season, 0–7–0. At least the Horned Frogs had put a few scores in their column in 1903, improving over their scoreless 1902 campaign. A few scores, though, could not lighten the pall that was stifling the program.

1904

Despite glimmers of improvement that began to show in 1904, the school's and administration's football morale continued to fall. C. E. Cronk gets credit in the modern TCU media guides for coaching the team in 1904,

Add Ran team, 1904.
The opening lineup in '04 was LE Howell Knight, LT A. J. Muse, LG Bonner Frizell,
C Ambrosia Martin, RG Stuart, RT Pete Wright, RE Arrington, LH Clyde Burnett,
QB Napoleon Grissom, QB Homer Rowe, RH Bailey, and FB Charles Ashmore.

but probably quit the task shortly into the season. The call went out in September for every able-bodied boy at TCU to try out for the team. The students responded, and the '04 team was a heavier, faster outfit than its winless predecessor. Senior tackle A. J. Muse, the team's captain, quarterbacks Hardy "Napoleon" Grissom and Homer Rowe, and fullback Charles Ashmore led the team.

Wacoans turned out in droves for the opening of the season, held at Baylor's field. The students cheered vigorously until the heat, atypical for mid-October, wore them out. It wore TCU's players out, too. They called for timeouts frequently, irking the Baylor players and fans. Baylor took pride in its players' better conditioning. It could not take pride, however, in a win. TCU was stout defensively, holding Baylor scoreless in the first half, even though the play was primarily near TCU's goal. After halftime, the play was primarily near Baylor's goal. The teams settled for a scoreless tie.

The next week TCU traveled to Austin to play the University of Texas for the first time since 1898, and suffered its worst loss since the Baylor blowout in 1901, losing 40-0. The *Skiff* called even this a moral victory, because fans expected the State school (as it was called in those early decades) to score even more. Amid the lopsided plays, lineman Bonner Frizzell garnered his first praise.

TCU took its 0-1-1 record to Fair Park in Dallas to meet the Fort Worth University Packers for the third game of the season, and lost a heartbreaker. The Packers ran around, through, and over TCU for the game's first few possessions, but did not score. TCU got into the act, with Arrington, Bailey, Napoleon Grissom, and A. J. "The Heavenly" Muse plowing to the Packers' two-yard line before the whistle for halftime. TCU blocked two field goal attempts in the second half, but the third—from the forty-yard line—was true. TCU missed its second-half field goal attempt, and lost 4-0.

TCU travelled again the next week to Texas A&M, glumly expecting another lopsided loss. Everything went wrong that could go wrong. Three starters did not make the trip, and those that did make the trip fell ill with food poisoning. To add insult to injury, the referees turned a blind eye to A&M's illegal formations and flagrant holding. The Aggies drove relentlessly, but won by a smaller than expected margin—29-0.

Dejected, the team finally got to play a game at home, again against Baylor, before about five hundred enthusiastic spectators. Baylor fumbled away its first drive, and TCU's Bertram Bloor, Bush, and A. J. Muse gained forty-five yards before fumbling possession back to Baylor. This time Baylor scored on a fifteen-play drive. On the second play of TCU's next drive, Muse galloped for thirty-five yards, only to see the Frogs fumble the ball away again a few plays later. The half ended after more fumbles and punts.

TCU opened the second half by driving within Baylor's five-yard line in ten successive rushes, but then the Frogs stalled and turned the ball over on downs. After a short Baylor possession, the Frogs again marched down the field in six plays and threatened to score, but were turned back once more on downs. This effort exhausted the Frogs, who gave up two more touchdowns on long Baylor drives before the day was over, losing 17-0. "The Heavenly" Muse tallied over eighty yards on seven carries—a banner day for the lineman.

By the time TCU and Baylor lined up to play for the third time in 1904, TCU had lost or tied eighteen consecutive games. The Horned Frogs were 2-21-5 since 1897, its only winning year on the gridiron. Their winning percentage (better termed "losing percentage") was .077 in that span, and they were outscored 421 to 57. The persistent losing had wrung the enthusiasm for football out of the pro-football administration that had allowed the sport back onto the campus in 1901. The board considered canceling the program in favor of TCU's very successful baseball team.

Would a win against Baylor in the season finale save football at TCU? Historically this was a tall order, but during the bye week before Thanksgiving Baylor lost three starters (Humphries, Wylie, and Milton) to injury. TCU again scrambled its backfield, with Clyde Burnett replacing Carpenter at right end, Fred Obenchain playing at left halfback for I. C. Harbour, and Harbour—who played the best game of his career—moving to right halfback for Bush.

On Thanksgiving Day the crowd was large, and the cheering done mostly by the coeds. They led the crowd in cheers such as

> Rak-ti-yak-ti-yak-ti-yak,
> rak-ti-yak-ti-yak-ti-yak,
> hullabaloo, hullabaloo,
> varsity, varsity, T-C-U

and

> Hi-rickety-whoop-ti-doo,
> Boomer! Sooner! T-C-U

and

> Rip! Ram! Bazoo!
> Rickety! Lickety! Zoo, zoo, zoo,
> Who, wah, wah, who,
> T-C-U!

and

> Yum! Yum! Fiddle-di-di-bum!
> Hump-stump flum-a-diddle
> Arum-bub-a-rigdum-jigdum—
> Bodi-modi-kiro-dilko-diro
> Yum! Yum! Fiddle-di-di-bum![30]

TCU kept the ball on Baylor's end of the field for the first half of the game, twice coming within a few yards of the goal. Harbour had runs of thirty, twenty, ten, fifteen, and ten yards, as well as several smaller rushes. There was a handful of fumbles by each team, but no scoring.

After trading drives several times in the second half—including one spurred by a thirty- or thirty-five-yard gain by H. H. Bryant, who subbed for Obenchain—TCU drove within the Baylor one-yard line, then turned the ball over on downs. Baylor made the puzzling choice to kick the ball almost from its own goal line, a kick Bonner Frizzell blocked. The ball fell across the goal line, and Ambrosia Martin recovered it for a touchdown—the Horned Frogs' first points of the season. The umpire did not allow the Frogs to attempt the points after, because he thought the ball touched the ground while in a TCU player's hand after the touchdown. The *Skiff* took exception, guessing that the umpire needed glasses, but the call stood and the game ended 5–0.

Finally the Frogs had a win—their first since 1901. The quality of the victory doesn't fully register in its score, as TCU outgained Baylor 327 yards to 78. The Horned Frogs' emotions soared, and the *Skiff* rushed

29

an insert into its weekly edition to crow about the win, completing its chest-thumping with the question, "And Baylor wants to play us again (?)" In one afternoon, victory—which seemed to have deserted the school for so long—had revived TCU's pride.

Beating Baylor in 1904 may have saved football at TCU. Doubts about whether TCU would play football again, against Baylor or any other team, suddenly vanished. Such a (statistical) trouncing—and of Baylor, no less—turned the administration away from its customary ambivalence about college football. Instead of cancelling the program, hampering it with travel restrictions, or simply ignoring the sport altogether, the administration stepped out of character and indebted Frog fans to the Midwest for a third time. In preparation for the 1905 season, TCU hired its first great football coach.

2
FLOURISHING

Trogs' winning seasons before the 1930s—if it characterizes them
at all—as exceptional seasons scattered on a background of losses.
Certainly this fairly describes the school's first decade of intercollegiate
football. But TCU's hiring of the Dallas lawyer and football coach Emory J.
Hyde altered the tenor of the tale. Far from a story of a few good years pep-
pering an otherwise bad dish, the story of TCU football, commencing with
the administration's recommitment to the sport in 1905, is a story of wins
and more wins, interrupted occasionally by a bad season. In the eighteen
seasons between Hyde's arrival and TCU's entry into the Southwest Conference, the Horned Frogs had a .532 winning percentage (seventy-four
wins, fifty-six losses, and nine ties), and outscored their opponents 2,105
points to 2,073. It is a proud, and largely forgotten, tale.

1905

E. J. Hyde was a Michigan man who played under, or perhaps with, Fielding Yost before practicing law in Dallas. Hyde had a knack for cultivating
teamwork from his players and peers. He instituted a charming tradition
of taking his varsity players, the team manager, and supportive professors
around town in a decorated horse-drawn carriage called a "tallyho."[31] The
first of these trips included a surprisingly talented cast of returning players for a team that had nearly been disbanded because of its mounting losses. Hyde's second-year players included future all-state performers Howell
Knight and Pete Wright and the solid veterans A. J. Muse, Fred Obenchain, Bertram Bloor, and Charles Ashmore. Among the freshmen were
future all-stater Blue Rattan and headliners T. B. "The Flying Terror" Gallaher. A good coach could build a good team with this kind of roster.

The team building showed on the field from the get-go. On an unseasonably warm day, in front of about a thousand fans including the "roota-
torial gangs" for each school, TCU trounced Baylor in the season opener.
It took Baylor twelve plays to stop the Frogs' first drive. While that drive
ended on a missed kick, TCU got the ball back quickly and drove the field,
Gallaher scoring on an end run to the right. The teams traded punts for
the remainder of the half. After a failed Baylor drive, the Frogs muscled
the ball down the field and scored on Gallaher's nimble thirty-yard run.
On TCU's first possession of the second half, Gallaher recovered a Baylor fumble and returned it seventy-eight yards before Baylor's King could
make the tackle from behind. A few plays later Blue Rattan scored his first
collegiate touchdown. A. J. Muse and T. B. Gallaher powered the Frogs to
a third touchdown, and the Frogs won 17-0.[32] Gallaher had 128 yards on
the day, on only three carries.

Gone were the *Lariat*'s expectations of an easy win over TCU. Instead,

Team photos, 1905. A mustached E. J. Hyde appears in the upper photo on the fourth row, and in the lower photo on the back row, second from left. Howell Knight, the team captain (on the third step in the top photo) is holding the ball in each picture.

the Baylor newspaper gushed, "Muse, TCU's big tackle, and Gallaher, her fast fullback, were the bright stars in that team. Their individual work, coupled with almost perfect teamwork, were the main features of the game from the standpoint of the victors."[33] News of the victory—considered an upset—registered in faraway places.

After a bye, the Frogs travelled to Austin, losing 11–0. Gallaher's speed, along with the strength of TCU's line, surprised the Longhorns. "Strange to say," the *Skiff* quoted the Austin *Democratic Statesman*, "instead of becoming discouraged [after the University of Texas drove the field and scored], TCU braced and proved marvelous in holding the Texas team in plunges against the line." On one twenty-one-yard run by Gallaher, "hats, umbrellas, and everything which was carried went into the air." Texas's size, claimed by the *Skiff* to be twenty pounds more per man, on average, than TCU's, was too much for the Frogs, but the locals went away from the 11–0 Texas win impressed by the Frogs' pluck. The *Skiff* quoted another Austin paper:

> It is a wonder that TCU, a young school with only a few hundred young men attending, and some of the team entirely new at the game, could have put up such a fine contest. The team had only been practicing about fifteen days, too, and yet they held the State University down better than any team has done in the past four years. In other words, they came nearer winning the game than any Texas team has come within four years. It was in reality a great victory for TCU.[34]

The fifteen players from Waco were not the only visitors to Austin that afternoon. Fielding Yost, who had come to Waco for a relative's funeral, had a second reason for making the trip—to see the Frogs play the Longhorns. TCU's win over Baylor had piqued his interest, explained the legendary coach, who sat atop the grandstand next to the editor of the *Skiff*—and besides that, Coach Hyde was an acquaintance. Yost went on to chide the *Skiff*'s editor, a big man, for not playing with the team.

After another bye, the Frogs travelled by train to Sherman to play the Austin College Kangaroos on a Friday afternoon. Early in the game the teams managed four fumbles on one play. The Frogs made an impressive goal line stand in the first half, and after gaining possession on downs, drove the entire field for the only score of the half. Gallaher missed a "difficult" point after. After trading punts and turnovers on downs, Gallaher kicked a field goal shortly before the first half expired, prompting one TCU professor Anderson to "uncork a few vials of his exaggerated enthusiasm."[35] Gallaher broke free in the second half for a sixty-five-yard

T. B. "The Flying Terror" Gallaher, from the 1905 yearbook.

touchdown run, and kicked the point after. TCU scored once more, finishing the game ahead 21–0.

Next, Texas A&M brought its affinity for end runs to Waco. TCU's score in the first half came on a lateral to Jones, who turned and handed off to fullback Gallaher. "The Flying Terror," as Gallaher was called, ran through the A&M line and hurdled the Farmers' renowned quarterback "The Indian" Kelley en route to the goal line—a ninety-yard sprint. The *Skiff* called it one of the greatest gains of all time.[36]

The game was penalty-free, and tied 6–6 at halftime. But by the time Napoleon Grissom broke free for forty-five yards on an end run late in the second half, A&M had scored 18 points, and the Frogs trailed 24–6. Six plays later Grissom gained twenty more, and A. J. Muse capped the drive with the last touchdown of the game. Bloor missed the point after in the gathering darkness. The game ended a minute early because it had become too dark to play, and TCU lost 24–11. Baylor's players attended to watch their rivals, taking notes of the Frogs' plays to inform their own practice prior to the crosstown matchup with TCU.

For the first of these two games against Baylor, TCU was banged up from its match with A&M. T. B. Gallaher only played the last few minutes of the game, and Grissom could not play after halftime. Baylor scored the only touchdown in the first half, but missed the point after; the score was

5-0 at halftime. The longest plays of the day were a forty-yard run around right end by TCU halfback Jones and a thirty-yard run by Muse after bucking through the Baylor defense, both in the first half. After the half, Baylor drove relentlessly down the field in short gains and scored the second goal in a seventeen-play drive; again Baylor missed the point after. Up 10-0, Baylor again drove toward TCU's goal, then it lost the ball. Baylor fans claimed the referee had already whistled the ball down, but ultimately the play was ruled a fumble. TCU now held the ball, and promptly drove seven plays for a score, Muse tumbling over the goal line. The Frogs made the point after, and the game ended 10–6. Baylor's fans taunted, "Baylor 10, Referee 6." Although the game was otherwise remarkably clean (there were only two fumbles), the editors of the *Lariat* remarked that TCU "showed her usual disposition to squabble."[37]

The largest crowd ever at Baylor's Carroll Field—twelve hundred fans, most of whom had never seen a football game before—came amid a cold spell to see TCU's second bout against Baylor. TCU received the opening kickoff and drove fifty yards on ten carries, only to fumble the ball away at Baylor's twenty-five-yard line. Regaining possession at its twenty on a Baylor fumble, Bertram Bloor started the Frogs' next drive with a thirty-yard run and a dizzying hurdle of a Baylor defenseman. The hurdle, however, did not net enough yards to convert, thus ending a thirteen-play TCU drive only inches from Baylor's goal. T. B. "The Flying Terror" Gallaher, A. J. "The Heavenly" Muse, Pete Wright, and Bush combined to carry the ball just four inches shy of the goal, but Baylor held and got the ball on downs. TCU's third drive failed with a fumble on Baylor's eight, and the half ended scoreless.

In the second half, Gallaher ran determined to reverse the Frogs' ill luck. He carried the ball four or five times in the Frogs' first drive, getting about thirty-eight of the drive's seventy-five yards, including carrying the ball over the goal line. Once there, however, he fumbled it—in those days a ballcarrier had to down the ball over the goal line in order to score—and Baylor's Buster recovered it, averting a TCU touchdown. Gallaher was not to be denied, however; with Bloor and Muse he drove the field, carried the ball into Baylor's goal again, and this time held on to it for a score. Gallaher and Muse added scores again in the second half, and Ambrosia Martin made multiple stops behind the line. TCU won 17–0 and took the season series with two victories to Baylor's one.[38]

TCU also lost to Texas A&M again, and beat Trinity, to finish the year 4–4. Those four wins were the most the Horned Frogs had ever tallied in a single season. E. J. Hyde had turned TCU's ship around. Fourth-year player Bonner Frizzell was elected captain for the '06 season by the '05 squad—a standard method of electing team leaders for upcoming seasons.

Howell Knight, team captain, 1905.

1906

The superb exhibition of ground-eating football that closed TCU's 1905 season exemplifies the oldest era of the game. Old American football was about punting, line play, playing both ways, and more than all else, about rushing the ball and the ballcarrier. This combat—largely without pads and helmets—was punishing. Sensational injuries and deaths on the football field fueled national outrage against the sport, which in turn prompted a revolution in the rules that would, in three spasms of rule changes over six years, beget modern football.

The initial problem facing the rules committee was how to discourage violent mass plays. Mass plays—unlike wedge plays—were attempts to gain yards through the defense by interlocking blockers for the purpose of pulling and pushing the ballcarrier. Mass plays were the soul of early football. How could the committee save the sport from its dangerous reputation without altering the game beyond recognition? The rules committee, in an effort headed by representatives from Harvard, did not directly outlaw the mass play, but tried to discourage it by allowing more open plays.

The resulting rule changes almost make a catalog of the modern rules: the distance required for a first down doubled from five to ten yards; offenses could not have more than five players in the backfield; the neutral zone was created; games were shortened to sixty minutes and the halftime break was instituted; penalties were introduced for hurdling, unnecessary roughness (defined as tripping, tackling out of bounds, and piling up), and personal fouls (including punching, kneeing, kicking, and "striking with locked hands by linemen breaking through").[39] Some of the new rules were short-lived: the number of players on the line of scrimmage was limited to six, and linemen lining up in the backfield had to line up more than five yards off center. The referees did not escape notice from the rules committee, which created a centralized board of referees and added an extra umpire to games (although the competing teams could agree to dispense with this requirement).

But the revolution, and the most enduring symbol of the 1906 and subsequent rule changes, was the legalization of the forward pass. This was not a green light for a modern passing game, but the rule revisions of 1906 allowed forward passes in a small set of circumstances. Walter Camp, who was still highly influential in football rule changes, despised forward passing and won heavy restrictions on it in the 1906 rule changes. Passes had to cross the line of scrimmage off center at least five yards, could only be caught by an end, were turnovers if incomplete, and could not be caught for a touchdown. (Imagine football without touchdown passes!) The ball, when passed out of bounds, belonged to whichever team recovered it first and was turned over if it touched an ineligible player. So forward passes, while allowed, could not be a focus of an offense. They were trick plays, gimmicks. The ball was more rounded, anyway, and was more difficult to control, so the passing game as a basic offensive tool remained impractical, as well as mostly illegal. Football's soul remained in its ground game.

Coach E. J. Hyde built TCU's 1906 team around a corps of experienced third-year players. These six—Bonner Frizzell, senior Howell Knight, Pete Wright, senior Ambrosia Martin, Bertram Bloor, and H. H. Bryant—were the first group of third-year players ever to play a full season at TCU. Blue Rattan, a second-year, was a key contributor, but not the star of the team. That role would be seized in the third game by a freshman—slight of frame but big in heart—named Noah "Cy" Perkins. (Contemporary accounts spell his middle name "Si," and refer to him almost exclusively by it.) Perkins is notable today as TCU's first quarterback to use the forward pass (completing the team's first pass in the last game of the season). To his contemporaries, however, Perkins was known as a remarkable punter and an utterly fearless tackler.

Noah Cushman "Cy" Perkins.

Perkins did not emerge, however, until well into the season. In the preseason scrimmage, Coach Hyde played Manley Thomas and Bryant Collins at quarterback. And it was fullback Paul Tyson, not Perkins, who turned heads in the opening practices.

Fort Worth University came to Waco for TCU's first game in football's new, open era, and to the surprise of the spectators, the game was penalty-free. The Fort Worth team, though a little lighter than the Horned Frogs, were better coordinated as a team. Baylor fans, whose school did not field a team in 1906, came out to cheer for the Packers, against their crosstown rivals.

TCU halfback Howell Knight tallied multiple gains over twenty yards, the longest a thirty-eight-yard scamper. TCU defended the forward pass

Weighing in at 120 pounds, Cy Perkins showed no fear tackling opponents nearly twice his size.

for the first time early in the second half; the Packers' Nies caught the pass from Mills for no gain. Mills's second forward pass, near the end of the second half, went for seven yards. The Frogs defended their first trick pass off of a fake kick in the second half, and the play went for no gain. The Packers managed the only score of the game in the final seconds, after a seventy-five-yard run by Mills. Pete Wright stopped the first line buck attempt to score, but could not stop the second as the clock wound down. TCU lost 6–0.

The following week, TCU traveled to Austin. It rained all morning and was cloudy all day, keeping the crowd thin for the match. The University of Texas team wore out TCU's eleven. Bonner Frizzell left the game before the whistle for the first time in his career. The two teams traded punts, the play moving always closer to TCU's goal, and when Texas blocked one of TCU's punts, it began a series only a few yards from TCU's goal line and quickly scored the game's first touchdown (but missed the point after). TCU held Texas from reaching its goal line after another wearying drive, but a second blocked punt gave Texas another short field. The Longhorns scored on the next play, and again missed the point after.

After halftime, Texas's Ramsdell rumbled for a thirty-yard touchdown, and finally Texas made its point after. Knight made a thirty-yard run of his own in the second half, but the Frogs could not capitalize on the effort. Texas scored the game's final points with ten minutes left to play. UT fumbled away both of its forward pass attempts, and both teams were penalized for hurdling—one of the new penalties under the rules. Texas won 22–0.

The loss at Austin was nothing compared to the pounding TCU took at College Station a week later. The *Skiff* said the Horned Frogs next to the Aggies were "like little pygmies unto the brawny giants."[40] The *Skiff* also reported that it usually took three Horned Frogs to down an Aggie. The lineup showed the Frogs' bruises: Wallace played instead of Dabbs at left guard; Cartwright played in Peters's usual place at left tackle, with Thomas filling Cartwright's usual place at left end; Perkins played quarterback; Tyson played Frizzell's position (halfback), and Reed and Harwood filled in for Tyson at fullback. Frizzell only played the last five minutes of the game.

The score did not dim Cy Perkins's remarkable debut as a defenseman. "To see a 120–pound quarter dive at a mountain in the shape of Ross or Cornell looked like a pity, but later to see the mountains tumble and the little fellow come out the victor, was great," raved the *Skiff*.[41] Pete Wright also showed his defensive potential, recording "six or eight" tackles for loss. TCU did try its first forward pass, from J. B. Frizzell. It was incomplete to Cy Perkins, resulting in a fumble that A&M recovered and ran over TCU's goal line; the score, however, was forfeited because of a penalty. TCU was shut out for the third straight game, 42–0.

What must the Horned Frogs have thought during the next two weeks, preparing for a rematch with A&M in Waco? They healed somewhat; Bonner Frizzell started again, but the game began poorly for TCU just the same. The Horned Frogs fumbled three times deep in their own territory in the first three minutes of the game. A&M was only able to turn the third of these fumbles into points. The teams battled to halftime, with the Farmers up 12–0. In the second half, TCU had memorable tackles for loss by Pete Wright along with dozens of punts by Cy Perkins, but still no points. The Frogs' fourth consecutive shutout ended 22–0.

The following week, TCU began a weird attempt at a home-and-home series with Daniel Baker College, in Brownwood. For the first scheduled match, TCU players travelled by train 120 miles west to Brownwood, arriving at 2:00 a.m. on Saturday, only to find themselves two miles from the lodging that Daniel Baker had arranged for them—a barn, with oat-filled pillows. The *Skiff* called it an "asinine environment."[42] In similar fashion, the playing field, "ideal for grazing," was thick with vegetation, rent with ravines and wallows, surrounded by barbed wire, and had a cannon facing it from one goal to intimidate visitors. The mosquitos were as big "as wolves" and behaved just as poorly as the townsfolk, who argued about the rules and may or may not have come to the game armed with knives and clubs to make sure the referees called no penalties against their team. Daniel Baker kicked one field goal while the officials were conferring, reported John Pyburn. Legitimate or not, the field goal was the game's only score. Daniel Baker won 4–0.

Bonner "Fritz" Frizzell,
team captain, 1906.

Not minding TCU's string of shutouts that Daniel Baker had pushed
to five, the *Skiff* issued a challenge to Daniel Baker:

> When you come up to Waco, Brownwood, we will treat you
> upon the erroneous assumption that you are college men.
> We will establish you in a first-class hostelry, and show
> you the streetcars and give you an unmerciful drubbing at
> clean, straight, college football—but leave your bullying and
> violence at home, Daniel Baker, else there may be a new
> version of the ancient story of Daniel in the lions' den.[43]

Perhaps the threat was credible, because Daniel Baker did not show
up. It forfeited the return game, giving as an excuse the *Skiff*'s report of
the game in Brownwood a week prior.[44]

Beginning with a victory over the Deaf & Dumb Institute the following week, TCU shed its losing streak and began its most successful
thirty-game stretch until the 1920s. Fort Worth University came to Waco
to finish its home-and-home with TCU. Against the Packers, Cy Perkins
completed a twenty-yard pass to Reed in the first half for the Frogs' first
completed pass. Tackle Albert Billingsly made his first start and made
multiple long end runs; Howell Knight averaged eleven yards per carry,
Billingsly seven, including three twenty-yard runs around the same end.
Pete Wright scored TCU's touchdown early in the game, and the Packers
answered in a drive featuring three consecutive twenty-yard pass plays.

The game was tied with about five minutes remaining before the half. In the second half a dog ran onto the field and into a play. The animal did not break the tie, but Howell Knight did, kicking a thirty-five-yard field goal for the winning points in the second half. TCU won 9–5. Its season record was poor, two wins and five losses; but Coach Hyde's team had set a winning foundation for the future. The Horned Frogs' first golden era had begun.

1907

Pete Wright played his way into the fore of those players who would return in 1907. Wright combined with Manley Thomas, John Pyburn, and Cy Perkins to form the nucleus of the 1907 team. John Pyburn began his starting career, and another Muse, this one not A. J., was elevated from playing center on the second team to playing with the first team at right tackle. Thirty-five players trained for spots on two squads.

The team and some boosters held a meeting of all the male students at the school shortly before the season and passed the bucket, raising a couple hundred dollars. TCU held a similar meeting at the close of the 1906 season, and the combined sums held by the school from the two meetings was about four hundred dollars.

A couple of familiar faces were on the field, in referee's stripes, for the season opener in Waco against the Fort Worth University Packers. The head linesman was Fred Obenchain, and one of the timekeepers was Bonner Frizzell. Former players and coaches appeared as referees regularly. Obenchain would repeat as a lineman. Frizzell appeared as a field judge for the first 1909 Baylor game. In 1908 then ex-coach Hyde was the referee for three TCU games, and was coldly referred to in the *Skiff* as Hyde "of Michigan" or "of Dallas," or not "of" anything at all.

The team held the Packers' offense to three and out on every drive of the 1907 season opener. Howell Knight prevented the Frogs from losing when the Packers' Slawson scooped up a fumbled ball and ran as far as the Frogs' fifteen-yard line before Knight saved the play with an open-field tackle. The game ended in a scoreless tie.

Baylor, which again fielded a football team after a year without one, first played the Frogs that year at Carroll Field. It was also the first game in which Baylor attempted something like a balanced attack of passes with runs. It had rained all of the previous day, making this first Baylor game of 1907 a muddy, fumbly affair, featuring lots of fifteen-yard penalties for incomplete passes. The crowd was thick, despite the weather. For some reason Baylor had a high opinion of its passing game but only completed four of eight pass attempts. Baylor did, however, make the most of those

Loy C. "Pete" Wright,
team captain, 1907.

completions, tallying 108 yards on four catches.

Lineman J. O. Wallace completed TCU's only pass, a twenty-yard strike early in the game. Baylor matched that feat, and added yards after the catch, with Robinson taking the ball twenty more yards to the TCU five-yard line before Manley Thomas could make the tackle. Three plays later, Robinson ran it in for the first score of either team's seasons. TCU fumbled away a long drive that got within Baylor's ten-yard line. A penalty pushed Baylor into its end zone, where it punted, and the ball struck the goalpost. Howell Knight scooped it up and ran it in for the tie.

In the second half Baylor twice blocked Will Massie's kicks. The game ended in a 6–6 tie, though Baylor out-gained TCU on the ground 255 yards to 96 and converted several more third downs than TCU. Of course, the Baylor paper thought its team was "decidedly" better. The *Skiff* showed greater maturity, calling the game "one of the finest examples of football that has been delivered in Waco for years" and praising all of the competitors' efforts, skill, and ardor.[45]

The Frogs' first trip out of Waco in 1907 took them north to Sherman, where TCU beat the Austin College Kangaroos soundly. After driving by line plunges and end runs to the Kangaroos' two-yard line, and turning the ball over on downs, "Big John" Pyburn blocked an Austin College punt, and Pete Wright recovered the ball in the end zone for TCU's first touchdown. The Frogs' next drive nearly stalled after progressing about forty yards with runs, but was revived by a successful onside kick. Manley Thomas ran eighteen yards for a score on the next play, and scored TCU's

Team photo, 1907.

second touchdown on the next drive. The younger Muse bucked the line for a fourth Frog score, and in the game's final minute, Cy Perkins galloped seventy yards for another touchdown. The final tally was TCU 27, Austin College 0. Because the Frogs were on the road, quite a few TCU students and fans watched Baylor shut out the Deaf & Dumb Institute in Waco instead. The game was notable to the *Skiff* because both teams "resorted" to forward passing.[46]

TCU shut out its next opponent, Waxahachie's Trinity Tigers, by the same score of 27–0 in a muddy game. The rout could have been worse, as the Tigers held TCU to a single touchdown in the first half, despite playing within their thirty-five-yard line much of the time. Three Horned Frogs scored four times in the second half, Pete Wright (twice), William Massie, and Howell Knight, and still the half felt like a punting duel to the *Skiff*. Such was the tenor of the age.

After a bye, TCU returned to Baylor's campus and won by one point. Cy Perkins passed five times, four times successfully. Three of those completions went to Manley Thomas, who turned them into gains of thirty, five, and twenty-five yards. Howell Knight and Thomas were injured and left the game. As TCU's line weakened with the injuries, Baylor's fortunes on the ground reversed, and Puett ran for two long touchdowns—one for eighty yards a step ahead of Bertram Bloor, and another for fifty-five. Perkins had a thirty-yard run, and Pete Wright would have had a forty-yarder but for a penalty that negated the run. TCU won 11–10, although the game ended in a full-blown controversy regarding a safety that the referee

45

Bertram H. Bloor (halfback, fullback) began playing for TCU in 1905.

did not award to TCU. Other officials at the game submitted written statements to a "competent authority" to assess the call.

Controversially or not, TCU had tasted winning, and loved it. The *Skiff* suspected a deity had come to stay in north Waco. The deity stopped its travelling in Waco, apparently, because the Frogs lost the following week at College Station, amid pools of standing water on the gridiron. Thomas and Knight did not make the trip either (perhaps a factor in the outcome); what they missed was apparently very entertaining. The *Skiff* reported that the spectators were "constantly kept in an uproar of laughter" by the multi-fumble skidding, diving scrums of wet players trying to secure the ball, or players falling into puddles on their posteriors (or, to quote a contemporary account, the "nether extremity of his backbone with his head and feet in the air") and spinning like tops.[47]

Bertram Bloor got his first start, at right halfback, as did M. C. Stewart at left tackle and Charles Fields at left guard. TCU only once answered A&M's speedy quarterback "The Indian" Kelly, who twice scored on long runs. Horned Frog A. M. Harwood intercepted Kelly in the first half and returned the ball forty-five yards for a touchdown Otherwise it was all A&M, all day. The Farmers scored twice in the first seven minutes and twice more before the break. TCU lost 32–5.

After rebounding with a 6–5 victory over Trinity, TCU again faced Baylor for the Thanksgiving finale. Despite the cold and wind, the match-up featured the largest crowd ever to watch a game in Waco. This season the record-setting crowd numbered about fourteen hundred spectators, some of whom crowded around the fence surrounding the field because all of the benches were full. In a pregame speech, Pete Wright exhorted his teammates, "Boys, you want to hit 'em so hard that it will jar their ancestors four generations back."[48]

Levy Ward, a backup quarterback for Baylor, played the game in his street clothes (he would not be the last Baylor player to beat TCU while out of uniform). Baylor moved methodically through TCU's line, and passed the ball for success. The only bright spots for TCU fans came on defense, where Pete Wright made his trademark tackles for loss and Manley Thomas had a sixty-five-yard punt return for a touchdown. Not to be outdone, Baylor also returned a punt for a touchdown, and won 16–8.

Despite the drubbing from Baylor, the Horned Frogs' season was a success. The year-ending loss was only one of two during the year, and the year's full record was four wins, two losses, and two ties—the first non-losing season for the Frogs since 1897. The Frogs' long losing decade had given way to winning.

Winning for TCU in 1907 began, as it has for winning football teams ever since, up front. Its starting line of left end Albert Billingsly, left tackle M. C. Stewart, left guard J. O. Wallace, center William Massie, right guard "Big John" Pyburn, right tackle Pete Wright, and right end Manley Thomas made the best squad of linemen yet to play for the purple and white (even if their uniforms were, in those days, blue). Three of them won TCU's first all-state honors: end Manley Thomas, tackle Pete Wright, guard John Pyburn. Quarterback Cy Perkins won the honor as well.

The 1907 season was E. J. Hyde's last year to coach at TCU. He returned to his law practice in Dallas, occasionally resurfacing as a referee in TCU football games. Other than a name on a few lines in the school's modern media guides, Coach Hyde is largely forgotten. But having led the team back to success under the old rules, and then to greater success under the early new rules that allowed a forward passing game, Emory J. Hyde deserves a name among the list of TCU's great football coaches. It is a monument to Coach Hyde and his remarkable players that the Frogs' winning ways long outlasted his tenure as coach.

1908

Seeking to replace Coach Hyde, TCU turned to his alma mater and hired another pupil of Fielding Yost. The young graduate, J. R. "The Little Corsican" Langley, was the second of Yost's pupils to coach at TCU and is Horned Frog football's fourth debt to the Midwest. The *Skiff* expected good things from the Michigan man, because he came highly recommend by Yost as a teacher of the game, and because TCU had so many return-

Manley Thomas, captain 1908.

ing players, including Blue Rattan, Bonner Frizzell, Cy Perkins, Manley Thomas, "Big John" Pyburn, and Will Massie.

The season opened with a shutout of the Deaf & Dumb Institute, although the *Skiff* didn't consider this a true test of the Frogs' mettle. That true test came at Carroll Field a week later, against Baylor, who played without its best tackle, Gant, and also without its coach, who had already missed several practices that week due to illness. Baylor could not get around Manley Thomas on end-arounds, or through the line up the middle on line bucks. Baylor never passed TCU's thirty-five-yard line.

The longest play of the day was a thirty-five-yard run by Howell Knight that set up TCU's first score. Four short runs later, end Ray Wakefield toted the rock across the plane. The point after was a double-kick, Cy Perkins punting to Thomas, who lateralled to Bertram Bloor, who kicked the goal. Baylor lost several fumbles, and TCU halfback Albert Billingsley completed a twenty-five-yard pass that the end, Knight, fumbled away. The two connected again in the second half for a twenty-yard gain, this time fumble-free. Bloor bucked through Baylor's line for the Frogs' second touchdown before the half. The only score in the second half was a TCU field goal, and the Frogs won the match 15–0.

The school felt like this was finally its year to win against the University of Texas. The Katy line agent agreed to charter a special train to ferry TCU students to Austin, provided that at least 165 make the trip, for $2 each. By lunch on the day he made the offer, more than 100 students had ponied up the money, and the agent lowered the price to $300 total for the train. The athletic association agreed to guarantee the fee, only to learn that no train would be available, and the trip was off. About seventy students took a night train anyway, and cheered on the Frogs in Austin.

The *Skiff* called the match "the most memorable struggle in the history of the institutions."[49] The Austin papers had repeatedly published that UT's players were smaller than TCU's, but when the teams met on the gridiron, the Longhorns were larger (but only by about six pounds each, on average). Ends Pete Wright and Ray Wakefield played the game of their lives, with Wright tallying tackles for loss and Wakefield blocking for TCU's long gains.

Cy Perkins's punting was sensational—he had punts of fifty, sixty, and seventy yards in the first half, and another fifty-yarder in the second. Texas's first score came, however, on a botched punt attempt. After almost twenty minutes of fruitless play near midfield (which included a fifty-yard punt return by Billingsly), Charles Fields snapped the ball to Perkins to punt, and the ball went over Perkins's head. The Longhorns recovered and ran it in thirty yards for a score.

TCU scored its first points against UT since their first meeting in 1897 in the second half of the game, on a field goal by Will Massie. After Texas punted away its answering drive, Ray Wakefield caught a forward pass for a fifty-yard gain, and two plays later the Frogs covered thirty more yards through the air. The third time was the charm, though, for Texas, as it eventually intercepted a TCU pass. TCU held UT on that possession, however, and after punting again, the Frogs held the Longhorns. But, lest luck be seen to favor the state team, UT's Dyer muffed the snap on a punt and was downed behind his goal line by Pete Wright and Snelson for a safety. At the final whistle the score, 12–6, favored the Longhorns.

Instead of the scheduled match with Oklahoma A&M on the following Saturday, the Frogs played Trinity on a Monday, nine days after the game in Austin. Pete Wright did not start. For seven minutes, it looked like the near miss in Austin had undone the Frogs. TCU kicked off to start the game, and Trinity's McCollum returned the ball thirty yards, the first play of a twelve-play drive ending in a touchdown for Trinity. TCU fumbled away the kickoff, giving the ball back to Trinity, which proceeded to score again on an eight-play drive. Fortunately for the Frogs, Trinity's kicker missed both points after. Trinity forced TCU to punt away its possession, and then ran out of luck. The Frogs' defense began to assert itself, forcing a fumble on the next play, and the tide slowly turned in TCU's favor.

After trading punts, TCU scored on a four-play drive highlighted by Howell Knight's twenty-two-yard run to halve Trinity's lead. Will Massie made the point after. Trinity held TCU at its goal line before the half, keeping a 10–6 lead at the break.

A few possessions into the second half, Trinity again held TCU near its goal. Massie missed a game-tying field goal from the twenty-two-yard line. After a myriad of punts in the gathering dark, the Frogs threatened the Tigers' goal a third time, when a thirty-five-yard run by Pete Wright and consecutive line bucks by Howell Knight and Bertram Bloor pushed the ball to Trinity's two-yard line. Bloor carried the ball over the goal line, but fumbled. Crossing the plane was not enough to score in those days; a player had to down the ball behind the goal line for a touchdown. Trinity avoided falling behind by pushing the ball back across the goal. Massie blocked Trinity's punt, which rolled back over the goal line, and Knight recovered it for the go-ahead score—TCU 11, Trinity 10. Massie missed the point after, and mistakenly time was called. Play would have resumed because the timekeeper realized his mistake, but it was too dark anyway, so the Horned Frogs' one point lead became the final score.

TCU lodged its second win in 1908 over Baylor in a close game, at the Carroll Athletic Field on Baylor's campus, in something of a fiasco. Having trailed all of the first half, TCU recovered its own punt (or fell on its own field goal attempt) behind Baylor's goal line, after the ball bounced off a player on the field—the umpire didn't know which team's player the ball bounced off of—and TCU's Knight fell on the ball for the winning touchdown. The score was 10–6.

The *Lariat* wrote: "It is a fact that has been proven, that the ball struck a TCU player on the back, and by the rules should have been given to Baylor on the spot."[50] The editor comforted his readers with a litany of statistics that showed Baylor performed better, the final score notwithstanding. Baylor ran for about twice as many yards per carry as TCU. Baylor used quite a few forward passes and fake passes, and punted from an unusual formation, trying to put the game away, but missed multiple field goals.

Pete Wright was back in action when Texas A&M came to Waco the following week, and he very nearly sent them back to College Station losers. The difference in the game was Will Massie's missed field goal in the first half. Both teams scored a touchdown in each half of the game, and attempted a field goal in the first half—but only A&M's went through the uprights. Cy Perkins was ill, and averaged only about half of his usual yardage per punt. The Aggies used forward passes early in the game— three in its first scoring drive—to frustrate TCU's defense, but not without some failures. Bertram Bloor's seventy-five-yard run after recovering a forced fumbled on an Aggie pass attempt was the outstanding play of the game. A&M won 13–0.

Next week's game at Trinity was supposed to be a hard-fought match ending in a close score. "Captain Berry's team are a hard playing, gritty bunch and no lopsided score may be expected," declared the *Skiff* after its

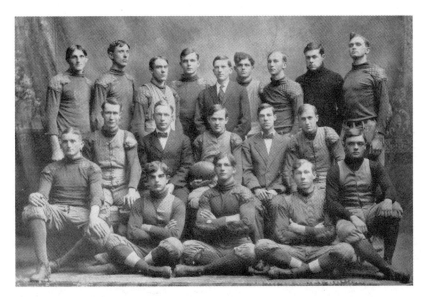
Team photo, 1908.

report of the A&M game.[51] TCU's team, on the other hand, lacked "pep," or "has not the life, the spirit that animated it during the first of the season." The *Skiff* urged the TCU players to "give all the spirit, the fire, the energy, and the strength that are yours" to the effort in Waxahachie.[52] These words were not wasted. Eight minutes into the game, Cy Perkins punted from midfield nearly to Trinity's goal line, and the Trinity player fielding the punt fumbled it. Will Massie recovered it on the four-yard line, and Albert Billingsly bucked across the plane on the next play. The teams mostly traded runs and punts for the remainder of the half, and the Frogs led 6–0 at the break.

Trinity collapsed in the second half, while TCU fielded a more open and varied attack. Trinity flubbed a punt on its first possession of the half from its own seven-yard line—the ball went straight up in the air and came down into TCU's possession on the eight-yard line. TCU scored two plays later. After trading punts, TCU scored a field goal, and on its next possession scored on an eighty-yard touchdown pass from Albert Billingsly to Marshall "Fuzzy" Baldwin. The Frogs substituted for most of their starters, which stopped Trinity's bleeding. The game ended 22–0—one of TCU's most dominating wins in its young history.

The next week TCU traveled to Georgetown to play the Southwestern Pirates for the first time. Southwestern, run by the Methodist church, had not been beaten that season, and had even beaten Texas. The Frogs played without their captain, Manley Thomas, and won without him 14–0, out-gaining the yellow- and black-clad Pirates 324 yards to 78 on the ground. Cy Perkins had returned to typical form, averaging about forty-one yards per punt. The Pirates frequently tried to pass for the advantage, but only completed three of fourteen passes for fifty-two yards.

For the finale against Baylor, TCU was at full strength, expecting Thomas to return to the lineup. TCU took its best-ever record of six wins and two losses to the match, and had already beaten Baylor twice. The game was really the first blockbuster match between the two schools, and would be the second to end in quasi-legal controversy. Baylor outweighed TCU and had a good punter, but the Frogs thought their lines and backfield were superior. What TCU lacked, however, was a good tailor, for the game would turn on a controversial uniform switch at halftime. The electric atmosphere featured students making a snake dance at halftime—that old tradition's first mention with TCU. The largest crowd to date came to watch the game, as the *Lariat* noted:

> The crowd on Thanksgiving Day was simply enormous. There were no vacant seats in the grandstands, the banks around the field were lined, and the vehicles encircled the field. Enthusiasm was at the very highest pitch and the yelling students, enforced by two bands, made the crisp air resound. College yells and songs were a specialty and the snake dance by the two hundred Baylor students to the music of the band between the halves was something new and interesting to the spectators.[53]

The Frogs drove eighty-seven yards on the opening possession to the Baylor eight-yard line, but fumbled away the promising drive. After trading several punts, Baylor's Robinson galloped forty yards for the game's first score. TCU answered with a drive over Baylor's goal line, but fumbled away the would-be touchdown in the end zone (a player still had to down the ball over the opposing team's goal line to get a touchdown). The Frogs, however, downed the Baylor player who recovered the fumble before he could race back over the goal line, netting a safety on the botched play. TCU missed two field goals before halftime, but Perkins scored a touchdown to give TCU an 8–6 lead before the break. The lead change undid the Baylor team.

Convinced it could not win, Baylor cheated. Its rising star end, Fouts, changed uniforms during the intermission, and emerged wearing TCU's blue in the place of Baylor's typical red, white, and gray. Baylor's coach refused to intervene when his opponents objected. He seemed to enjoy the ruse. Baylor tried to laugh off the deception, calling it "the oldest trick in the book."[54] Its results belied the excuse. Baylor's first play from scrimmage was a forty-yard toss to Fouts, the first of a nine-play scoring drive for the team. TCU's Albert Billingsly later "calmly" passed to Fouts for an interception. Fouts fielded punts while the Frogs blocked his teammates, and TCU's Ray Wakefield blocked for Fouts on one play. Baylor's quarterback wasn't always sure whether or not to give Fouts the ball. Baylor scored three touchdowns, all of the points in the second half, and won 23–8. The *Skiff* sent letters to various football coaches in the state, seeking their opinions about the legality of Fouts's uniform change at halftime. The replies were unanimous in condemnation, one coach calling it "dirty sportsmanship" beyond even the consideration of the Rules Committee. The *Lariat* did not even see fit to mention the event in its report of the game.

So TCU's season ended with six wins and three losses. To celebrate, the athletic association gave letters (called "monograms") to the players, coach, and manager. The letters were white, on purple sweaters. These may have been the first actual letter awards given to the football team.

In a lengthy piece for the *Skiff*, Coach Langley chose an all-Texas team by sorting through all of the Texas football programs (UT, TCU, Texas A&M, Baylor, Southwestern, Austin College, and Trinity). His team included end Manley Thomas, tackle Pete Wright, guard John Pyburn, and quarterback Cy Perkins. Coach Metzenthler of UT made an all-Southwestern team, and included only one TCU player, Pete Wright, at second-team left tackle.

Cy Perkins, star of the gridiron, the baseball diamond, glee club, and class president, had planned to go to Michigan for the 1909 year, and doubtless had many plans beyond that. But he died in 1910, the first of TCU's football greats to cross the plane of the great end zone in the sky. The school passed a resolution in memoriam.

1909

Coach Langley returned to coach the 1909 team, and faced the task of replacing Knight, Perkins, Bloor, Tyson, and Frizzell. Manley Thomas and Aubel Riter prepared to take over for Perkins at quarterback. The coach had high hopes for end Blue Rattan.

Langley's new team opened the season against a new Fort Worth foe, Polytechnic College, run by the Methodist Episcopal Church South. TCU clobbered the "Polys" 42–0, scoring five times before halftime. Halfback Paul Tyson ran forty yards for the game's first score and sixty more for TCU's final score of the half; in between, fullback Milton Daniel ran for three more. (When the Methodists founded Southern Methodist University in Dallas in 1911, it planned to convert Polytechnic College into a women's college—the forerunner of Texas Wesleyan University—at the

Paul "Ty" Tyson (fullback, halfback, 1905-1908) also played baseball for TCU.

same time. That conversion was completed in 1913, effectively taking the "Polys" red and black out of the current of football history. The school became coeducational again during the Great Depression, but did not resume playing football.)

Coach Langley tweaked the lineup for TCU's match with Texas A&M the following week. He switched John Pyburn and Mullican at right and left guard, and played Thomas at quarterback instead of Aubel Riter, who was intimidated by the A&M crowd. The game—a scoreless tie—was called a bigger victory for TCU than its rout of Polytechnic. Will Massie missed a field goal, the Frogs' only threat to score. The *Skiff* reporter claimed the game so interested him that he forgot to take notes after the first fifteen minutes.

The season's first match with Baylor was hard fought. Quarterback Thomas threw an interception for his first pass, but was perfect through the air thereafter, throwing twice more to Fuzzy Baldwin, for forty-five and eleven yards, respectively. He wrenched his knee, however, and did not play the next two games. Will Massie missed TCU's first kick attempt; Baylor blocked his second, and he made his third from the twenty-yard line to put TCU up 3–0. Shortly before the half Baylor moved the ball for a first down on TCU's five-yard line, but failed to score in three consecutive line plunges by Grissom, Willie, and Robinson. With only a few minutes remaining in the game—the score still 3-0—Baylor's Grissom kicked the ball onside, but TCU's Fuzzy Baldwin recovered it and scrambled sixty-five yards for the score. TCU won the game 9–0.

Austin College came to Waco the next week to face the Frogs. Riter was back at quarterback in Manley Thomas's place and led the team to an 18–3 victory. Charles Fields, Milton Daniel, and Paul Tyson each scored touchdowns—Tyson's on an interception return. Unsatisfied with the victory, the *Skiff* chided the team for allowing Austin College to score on them after three straight shutouts.

At Austin the next week, University of Texas humbled TCU with a 24–0 rout. Y. Armen Yates started for Mullican at left guard (Mullican latter subbed in). G. P. Braus played again at right halfback. The Frogs had driven resolutely to the Texas three-yard line as the first half expired, but otherwise were thoroughly stymied.

The second tilt in the annual trio with Baylor followed. Both teams came to the contest with injury-depleted squads—end Blue Rattan and guard John Pyburn were out for TCU, and quarterback Manley Thomas played despite a bum knee that had kept him out the last two weeks. Robinson, Baylor's captain, did not play. The game was scoreless at the half. Fuzzy Baldwin had the game of his life, hauling in five passes (three from Thomas, two from Massie) for ninety-two yards and a score, running the ball six times for about twenty-five yards, fielding a punt, and recovering a fumble and running it ninety yards for another score. TCU won 11–0.

Baldwin did not start the next week for the team's trip to Dallas against Southwestern, but he substituted and again was the outstanding pass catcher of the game, hauling in two passes for thirty yards as well as blocking a punt. Pete Wright scored the only touchdowns of the game—one on a three-yard plunge and the other on a blocked punt that he recovered over the Pirates' goal line. Thomas returned six punts and kicks for almost twelve yards per return. TCU won in a muddy shutout that was not as close as the 12–0 score indicates.

Much like the previous season's finale, the Frogs came to 1909's closing game against Baylor riding a high winning percentage. Baylor, however, would not be intimidated. It hosted a big bonfire Wednesday night prior to the Thanksgiving matchup, complete with a war dance. For the first time, attendance at the Baylor-TCU game topped two thousand.

Baylor had its captain Robinson back for the game, and he scored all of Baylor's points. Robinson proved to be the difference in Baylor's turn of fortunes in the second half of the season. More importantly, his punting kept TCU at bay. Will Massie scored a field goal on the Frogs' first drive, which had been extended with two passes from Thomas to Baldwin, for twenty-two and twelve yards respectively. TCU's left end Tom Lamonica and Baylor's left halfback Robinson traded punts the remainder of the half, which ended 3–0 in the Frogs' favor.

The punting duel continued about halfway into the second half until G. P. Braus fumbled, giving Baylor a short field. Baylor passed twenty-four

John "Big John" Pyburn, guard, started playing for TCU in 1908.

William "Bill" Massie, center, started playing for TCU in 1907.

yards to Isbell, and then scored two plays later on short runs. Robinson punted fourteen times, averaging just over thirty yards per punt. TCU's Lamonica punted twelve times (and one onside kick for forty yards on a fake run play), averaging two yards better. Neither team scored again, and Baylor won 9–3.

Blue Rattan (who would later attain the rank of general in the US Army) began a three-year hiatus away from school and football; he would return to TCU in 1913. Finishing the year 5-2-1, the Frogs elected Will Massie as captain of the 1910 squad, never guessing that they'd already played their last home game in Waco. In almost every sense, the team's and school's opening chapter had finished. Shortly after the '09 season, Coach Langley took a position in Oklahoma. Langley's departure marked the end of the Frogs' first brilliant run on the gridiron. The world would convulse in war before the Frogs would match the success of the Hyde-Langley years.

3
PANTHER CITY

During the week of the second game with Baylor in 1908, TCU had installed a hose to the water pipes in the main building in case of a fire. The nearest fire station was over a mile away, and the *Skiff* noted that without proper protection against fire, the building would likely be fully aflame before the fire department could arrive on site, if need arose.

The need did arise shortly after 8:00 p.m. on Tuesday, March 22, 1910. Roommates Roy Tomlinson, a football player, and Carl Melton, likely not a football player, discovered fire in the ceiling near their fourth-floor room in the main building. They and other boys tried to extinguish the blaze with buckets of water from the sink, while students on lower floors scrambled to save their books and furniture, some by throwing them out of windows. Tom Lamonica's efforts exhausted him, and he had to be carried to a pastor's home two blocks away.

No lives were lost (although one coed was struck by a falling trunk), but the building was completely destroyed. Only its stone outer walls remained after two hours. All the students could do was sit nearby with hundreds of onlookers and watch the conflagration. At about 10:00 p.m. the roof fell in, causing flames to rise two hundred feet into the night sky. The 1908 fire hose did not seem to have been used, although local firefighters did douse the nearby Girls' Home and Townsend Hall to prevent further fire. They succeeded too much, flooding the ground floors and adding considerably to the damage. The library—which contained six thousand volumes—two laboratories, classrooms, TCU's business office, dorm rooms for 175 male students, and a few faculty apartments were destroyed, although most of the business and enrollment records were saved from the business office. The destruction to the Main Building was valued at $120,000 to $150,000 over the value of the building's insurance coverage.

Locals took in the now-homeless boys. Some students grouped together and rented local homes. Class was suspended only for a day while TCU's president Clinton Lockhart and business manager James Anderson arranged for classes to be held in evacuated dorms in Townsend Hall and the Girls' Home, professors' homes, their own homes, and even outside. Not one student left the school that semester.

The university's attractiveness to other cities in north and central Texas seemed to weigh heavily, if unspoken, on the local spirit. Local civic and business leaders were immediately and profusely helpful; booksellers donated some replacement books for the library; the local Business Men's Club appointed a special committee to collect bids from locals to help replace the burned building. Businessmen met with TCU trustees, and spoke at a large gathering of TCU students in the gymnasium, courting the school's loyalty to Waco. The Baylor band, the superintendent of Waco public schools, the county judge, and *Tribune* editor George Robinson

Illustration from the *Horned Frog*, 1908.

attended a rally for TCU the night following the fire, at which Robinson announced that Waco could raise at least $50,000 toward reconstruction of the Main Building. The offer was, in Dr. Colby Hall's recollection, "hearty, but vague."[55] During the week, Baylor made its library and labs available to TCU, and Baylor's baseball team earmarked the proceeds from two exhibition games for TCU's rebuild.

Their zeal was met with politeness and gratitude from TCU's administrators, but also with patience and expressions of duty to seek the best interest of the school. The message could not have been clearer: TCU found in its ashes an opportunity for a new beginning. Waco's offer of $50,000 was quickly met and bested by offers from Dallas, Sweetwater, McKinney, Gainesville, and Fort Worth. Waco was losing the bidding war. Civic leaders, including the mayor, implored TCU's trustees to keep the school in town, saying TCU was morally bound to remain in Waco, which had done so much for the school for fifteen years. They increased their bid to $75,000 but could not come near the bids from Dallas and Fort Worth. Although partial to familiar Waco, the students finished the school year knowing that their schooling likely would resume in another city.

The offer from the civic boosters in Dallas was very attractive, but the boosters' simultaneous negotiation with the Methodists to open a university in Dallas rubbed TCU's administration the wrong way. The double-dealing swayed them toward the offer from Fort Worth. That leaders in Dallas and Fort Worth negotiated so intently for TCU indicates that the North Texas leaders knew that the young Fort Worth University was not thriving. FWU, on the present site of Paschal High School, was run by the Methodist Episcopal Church, and had a law school and a medical school. The school withered with the competition from TCU, and eventually merged with Epworth in Oklahoma City, which, in turn, eventually became Oklahoma City University.

Double dealing aside, TCU's students and faculty were hoping to move to Dallas. But Fort Worth's offer—including a fifty-acre campus with electricity, gravel road, streetcar, and sewer service—with a $200,000 cash bonus (to be raised by the Board of Trade, Christian Churches, and the sale of lots through the Fairmount Land Company by July 1) won the day. TCU began its tenure in Fort Worth housed in the Ingram Flats, a series of two-story brick buildings at the corner of Weatherford and Commerce that the school leased for $5,000 annually.

The Fort Worth to which TCU returned in 1910 could hardly have been more different from the dusty frontier outpost that it left behind during the Panic of 1873. The doldrums of that depression desolated the town economy so thoroughly that, according to local lore, a panther had strolled into town and taken a nap on the street, giving rise to the nickname "Panther City."[56] The nickname far outlasted the depression.

The malaise lifted on July 19, 1876, when the railroad came to town, arriving just before lunch, to an immense crowd of curious, and then jubilant onlookers. Many had camped overnight to see the steam engine roll into town. Fort Worth underwent a second transformation when two titans of the meat packing industry moved there in 1901. From 1900 to 1910, Fort Worth's population increased 275 percent to 73,312. Railroads proliferated; natural gas and electricity were in wide use by 1910, cluttering the town with utility poles. The Southwest's first metal rolling mill was established in Fort Worth in 1904.

The town had built a library, partly funded by Andrew Carnegie, and a large city park. It had condemned all of the wood buildings on Main Street, and supported multiple newspapers. The *Record-Register* (itself the combination of two antecedent rags) was the morning paper, and the *Fort Worth Star* (employing an ad salesman named Amon G. Carter) and the *Telegram* competed for afternoon readers until both folded at the close of 1908, and reopened on January 1, 1909, as the *Star and Telegram*.

Civil society had flourished since the Clarks left in the 1870s: the Masons and Eastern Star orders were advancing, and the Knights of

Pythias, Odd Fellows, Elks, Knights of Columbus, Boy Scouts, United Charities (B'nai B'rith), YMCA, and YWCA all had chapters in Fort Worth. The Southwestern Baptist Theological Seminary came from Waco to Fort Worth in the same year that TCU made its move. Roads still remained mostly unpaved; the road to TCU's campus southwest of town was not paved until 1923. Traffic on the roads was increasingly automotive, but driving in the early 1900s was not a routine exercise. Headlights were not electric; they were gas lanterns that had to be lit with matches, and easily blew out. Drivers and passengers fought rain and dust with clumsy curtains, goggles, extra clothing, hats, and tireless effort. In 1903, a party of prominent Texans set a speed record for driving from Dallas to Forth Worth in ninety-five minutes.

In 1909 Fort Worth hired its first traffic cop, who set up the town's first speed trap on West Seventh, using a stopwatch to measure cars' speeds on an eighth-mile distance. He learned to recognize the owners of cars by the sounds their cars made. The Fort Worth Fire Department had two fire trucks when TCU came to town; the rest of its work was still done with horse-drawn vehicles (with atypically intelligent horses, including one named Dewey who could unlatch his stall and gallop away, returning only when the fire bell rang). The police, however, were still unmotorized.

Streetcars ran through town, and folks congregated in any number of saloons, bars, and restaurants, including the landmark White Elephant which featured a forty-foot bar. Fort Worth's cinema—the Odeon—opened in 1910; admission to a one-reel film cost five cents.

Football was changing almost as fast as Fort Worth. Its rules evolution lurched ahead again prior to the 1910 season. Much like the famous 1906 conferences that ushered in the forward pass, the changes in 1909 were prompted by a rash of severe injuries and deaths on the gridiron, mostly caused by the violence of mass plays.[57] The 1906 rule changes attempted to impose some restraint, but chaotic mass plays continued to cause injuries and deaths. In 1909 the rules committee completely outlawed mass plays, making pulling or pushing the ball carrier illegal, and also forbidding interlocking blocking. Flying tackles were outlawed as well; tacklers now had to have at least one foot on the ground.

In other ways, however, the new rules beefed up the ground game. The quarterback was finally allowed to run with the ball, and ball carriers could now plow straight ahead instead of having to veer a few years off center before crossing the line of scrimmage. Seven players on offense had to be at the line, and crawling with the ball was prohibited. The two halves of the game were divided again, resulting in four quarters. And field goals were reduced to the present value of three points.

Beginning with the 1910 season, forward passes could cross the line of scrimmage anywhere (instead of outside the center at least five yards).

More players could be eligible receivers: now backs and ends could catch passes. Pass interference was introduced: incomplete passes on first and second downs were no longer turnovers. Passing was still restricted, though, compared to the modern game. The passer had to be at least five yards behind the line, and the eligible receiver could not be more than twenty yards beyond the line of scrimmage. The full unleashing of modern passing in football would come three years later.

The changes made in 1910 refined and consolidated the 1909 rules. The experiment with the forward pass had succeeded so well that the newest rules further encouraged aerial plays. Two-dimensional offense had arrived, and was here to stay. Football's infant soul—the lusty, dusty struggle for ground yards—was giving way to the modern game.

The rules revolution that created modern football finally ran its course prior to the 1912 season. This last burst of new rules primarily concerned passing. The size of the ball was slightly reduced, and its shape elongated, to make it easier to throw. End zones were added, and the field shortened, to allow for newly legal touchdown passes. Finally, passes were allowed more than twenty yards over the line of scrimmage. The fourth down was also added, and the points awarded for touchdowns and extra points reached their modern totals of six and one. The only major rule changes remaining in the formation of the modern sport were the substitution rules, which would not reach their present form for decades.

1910

The catastrophic fire and subsequent relocation took their toll on TCU's football team. The first two years back in Fort Worth gave TCU football its worst two-year record until after the Second World War (6-11-1)—although a new coach, Kemp Lewis, and some active recruiting promised better things to come. The athletic council chairman, C. I. Alexander, who had played for TCU's inaugural team in Waco, wrote a warning in the *Skiff* that students wishing to play on the football team had better be in class from the opening day of the term (September 14) "ready for the best year's work of [their] lives."[58] Team captain Will Massie and the manager toured a few high schools in the Dallas area (Dallas, McKinney, and Forney) to try to convince the better players from those schools to attend TCU. This recruiting trip, called "prospecting" at the time, is the first known mention of TCU actively recruiting for the sport, instead of passively waiting to see who showed up at the first practice after classes began. The recruiting trip netted Redwater Anderson, Ralph McCormick, and Clinton Swink—a success by any standard.

Turnovers marred the Horned Frogs' first home game in Fort Worth,

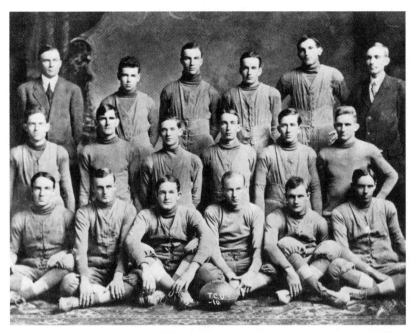

The 1910 team. Milton Daniel is third from left, back row.

held in Heinz Park, against Polytechnic. Poly coughed up the kickoff, giving TCU a short field and, in sixty-one seconds, a touchdown by Milton Daniel. But the red and black did not back down, and after a confidence-gaining twenty-yard completion through the air, Poly held TCU scoreless for the remaining forty-seven minutes of the game (the quarters were only twelve and a half minutes each). Late in the third quarter, Poly blocked two TCU kick attempts, eventually gaining possession at about midfield. After trading turnovers, Poly found itself in a third and long at TCU's twelve, but tied the game on a well-executed play-action pass. TCU threatened to retake the lead in the fourth, but tackle Charles Fields fumbled when tackled by two defenders at Poly's six-yard line. Poly promptly fumbled away the ball, and TCU returned the favor with a failed pass attempt, giving Poly possession to end the game 6–6.

The next week Texas A&M routed TCU in College Station, 35-0. A&M pulled its starters, then put them back in. The game took a lasting toll on the team: William Rattan (not Blue) dislocated his shoulder; Clinton Swink also was hurt and could not play the next week. The hitting was so intense that Henry Lavender's parents forbade him to play the game. He would return to the gridiron in later seasons.

In addition to injuries and parental objections, two starters for TCU—

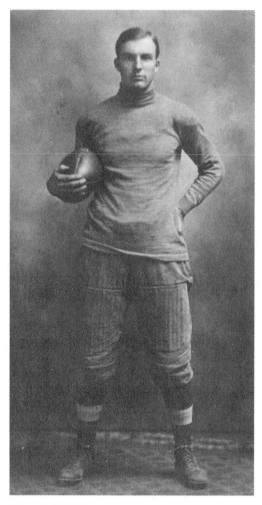

Milton Daniel, 1912.

Fields and Ralph McCormick—could not play against Baylor because of illness. The short-handed team that travelled to Waco for the first meeting between the once-sister schools was woefully outplayed by Baylor. Baylor fans chanted, "Add Ran's gone," and Baylor players played like a weight had been lifted from their shoulders, gobbling up yards by the dozen. TCU took to the air to try and staunch the rout—only to see Baylor's Robbie intercept two throws and return them ninety-five and forty yards, each for touchdowns. TCU converted third downs only twice, and the referee called the game with eight minutes remaining on account of darkness—or out of mercy—with the score 52–0.

Trinity came from Waxahachie to try to capitalize on the Frogs' recent slump. The *Fort Worth Record* predicted that Trinity could win only if its end runs were superb; they weren't. Blue Rattan and Ralph McCormick stuffed the Tigers' end runs throughout the game. Trinity muffed a fake kick in the first quarter, giving Clinton Swink the ball with five blockers; he easily scored the game's first points. William Rattan scored once and had two thirty-five-yard runs (one was called back for a penalty). The Tigers tried another fake kick later in the game. This time the Tigers' quarterback passed over the Frogs' defense for a score. Charles Fields scored TCU's third touchdown on a line buck in the fourth quarter.

The Frogs hazarded their 1-2-1 record against A&M again, this time in Fort Worth. From the get-go Coach Lewis could not stir his players to face the Farmers with much gusto, and again the purple and white lost, this time by only sixteen points. TCU missed tackles and blocks frequently, A&M rarely. TCU's score came in the game's final minutes, and for a minute TCU looked like it would score another, until it fumbled the ball away at A&M's five-yard line. Milton Daniel's play was a revelation. He averaged over forty yards per punt, and was TCU's soundest tackler. Late in the game he tackled both A&M's fullback carrying the ball, and his blocker. Ralph McCormick at end played solidly as well.

TCU played its return game with Trinity in Waxahachie, and broke the 0–0 tie in the fourth quarter with a long touchdown pass to Milton Daniel. Massie kicked a field goal for the other score of the game, TCU winning 9–0. The next week, on the road again to face Georgetown, TCU coughed up multiple interceptions—one for a score—but lost to Southwestern 25–3.

TCU made brave noises about beating Baylor, which expected to close as the season champions of the TIAA. Baylor's coach did not even attend the game, preferring instead to scout Southwestern in its match with A&M. His players protested that their accommodations in Fort Worth, at a YMCA instead of in a hotel, were subpar and prevented them from getting a solid night's sleep prior to the game. Because of construction at Heinz Park, the teams met at Butz Park on the north side of town. Mindful of the shellacking his team received from Baylor at the season's open, Coach Lewis moved Will Massie from center to end for the game, hoping to capitalize on his team captain's mobility both in blocking and as a ball carrier. William Rattan, who had not played since the second loss to Texas A&M, was expected to play.

TCU's crowd came to life when Milton Daniel returned the kickoff thirty yards—all ahead of his blockers. But the Frogs' drive stalled, and when Baylor got the pigskin on downs, it quickly drove for a score, and then another. Down 10–0 to open the second quarter, Daniel again assert-

Gildersleeve

The 1910 Thanksgiving Day game.

ed himself with a thirty-yard run, and the game settled into a defensive slugfest. Will Massie missed a field goal in the third quarter, but made one in the fourth. TCU lost 10-3. Milton Daniel and William Rattan drew praise from the *Lariat*, and the *Fort Worth Record* called Daniel's play his best yet at TCU.

After a bye, TCU finished the year on the road for Thanksgiving, playing Epworth University in Oklahoma City. Epworth was the underdog but outplayed TCU and won handily. Will Massie was knocked out of the game, which ended 30–0. The team ended its first season in Fort Worth in a funk that it would not shake for a season yet.

1911

A new coach, Henry Lever, led the team for the 1911 season, which began with unusually hot weather. Bolstered by a preseason pep rally, school spirit ran high. The athletic council expected the team to number as many as forty boys, who were likely to be smaller on average than their opponents. Returners Charlie Fields and Redwater Anderson were expected to anchor the squad. A transfer from Fort Worth University, which had moved to and merged with Epworth in Oklahoma City, Bryan F. "Bun" Ware found a place on the line at guard. Bun Ware had been captain of his teams in high school and at his first college.

Coach Lever could not secure any practice games with other local

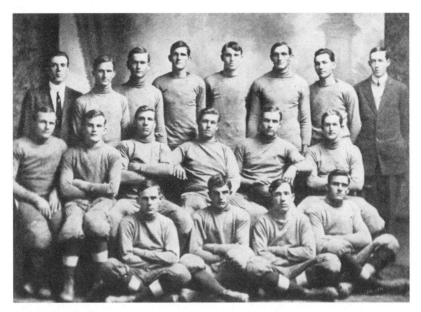
The 1911 varsity team.

teams; the Carlisle Military Academy in Arlington and the Arlington Independents both scheduled scrimmages with the Horned Frogs only to cancel them. The cancellations continued into the season when UT's football coach Wasmund died unexpectedly before the season opener, which was cancelled as well.

John P. Cox, from Hillsboro, and Tom Lamonica each had long runs in preseason scrimmages, but the lack of good-on-good practice with another team did not bode well for the season. Further darkening the outlook for 1911, Milton Daniel was hurt in a scrimmage and had to play for the scrubs; Bun Ware took his place at fullback for the remainder of the preseason drills. Optimism about the season had waned; the *Skiff* pleaded for students to cheer the team on at practice.

The season opener against the Trinity Tigers was hardly a fair fight: Trinity punted away many of its possessions on first down. John P. Cox, Clarence Bussey, and Bun Ware had most of the carries for the Frogs. One of Cox's went for fifty yards, but the Frogs failed to score on the drive. The Tigers showed more moxie on defense than offense, forcing TCU to turn the ball over on downs repeatedly in the first half. Trinity moved the ball offensively for the first time in the second quarter—twice using forward passes—but failed to score. Despite a wide disparity in yards, Trinity only trailed 6–0 at the half. After the half, TCU began to turn yards into points. John P. Cox scored three more touchdowns and T. C. Graves added a fourth. TCU won 30–0, but would not win again in 1911.

The first loss of the year came in Georgetown the following week, against a Southwestern player named R. K. "Mac" McHenry that TCU simply could not tackle. He eluded the Frogs all day, and led the Pirates to a shutout victory over TCU. A week later, the team lost for the first time to Austin College. Austin College was beginning its golden era of football and beat many others teams for the first time in 1911. TCU went next to Sherman to play the Kangaroos without Tom Lamonica, and seemed poorly conditioned to boot. TCU tackled poorly, allowing four end runs for touchdowns, each run for at least fifty yards.

TCU's next loss, also on the road, was more competitive. It did not come against A&M, as originally scheduled, but rather came in Waco, against Baylor. Both teams tried to throw the ball in the first half, without success. Baylor scored the only points of the half; TCU's John P. Cox missed two field goals in the third quarter. TCU also missed a would-be touchdown by Tom Lamonica who, while running in the open field towards Baylor's goal, fell "on account of previous injuries."[59] The only remaining score of the game came in its final minute, after the sun had set. TCU lined up for a third field goal attempt in darkness so thick the ball could not be followed after it was kicked. Baylor caught the short kick, and with pitches and runs got the ball into the hands of its best player, Fouts, who ran it in for a touchdown. Baylor won 12–0.

The Frogs' losing streak reached a disappointing four against Austin College in Fort Worth—disappointing because the Frogs did not seem outplayed by the Kangaroos, but lost anyway. Returning after an injury, Milton Daniel played, but not in top form. Oscar Wise and Bug Thannish were playing out of position. Quarterback Clarence Bussey missed three of four throws in the first half, giving up an interception shortly before the whistle. Both teams scored a touchdown in the first quarter—TCU's coming on a blocked punt that Charles Fields ran in for a score. Austin College tried a triple pass in the game, but it was called back for holding. The Frogs made a field goal and took an 8-6 lead to halftime, but allowed a touchdown in each of the third and fourth quarters, in an otherwise punishing game of punts and fruitless ground gains. The Kangaroos won, 18–8.

The season finale featured Polytechnic. Despite an interception sparking a long Polytechnic drive, TCU held off the Polys for the first quarter. After a punting battle featuring six punts and a missed field goal, Poly blocked the seventh punt attempt, and recovered the ball behind TCU's goal line for the game's first score. The Polys scored again before TCU got on the board with a field goal shortly before halftime. At the whistle that ended the season TCU was down 16–3, and had been outscored 106–41 for the year. The Frogs hadn't performed so badly since their coachless days at the turn of the century.

TCU's modern media guides mention three games to close the season, one versus a high school and two with Southwest Oklahoma. These games do not appear in contemporary records, and likely never happened.

Milton Daniel, Oscar Wise, and Bozeman were the only players lost to graduation in the spring of 1912. The team elected Bun Ware captain for the coming season, when the Frogs would smash many of their football records.

1912

Bun Ware and his teammates expected to play another season for Coach Lever, and with the final rule changes in the books, expected to play the most wide-open football ever at TCU. But when the call went out in the fall for players to report, Willis Stewart had been hired as coach. Stewart, a Vanderbilt alum, had coached one year at a school in Mississippi and was active with the YMCA. He assumed the reins of a program that had acquired two dozen new uniforms—gray jerseys, moleskin pants, and purple and white socks. These uniforms may have been TCU's first sporting of the color purple.

September 6 was named the day to report for practice. The roster of returners was long and illustrious: ends William Rattan and Lester "Bug" Thannish, quarterback Charley Bussey, tackle and fullback Bun Ware, tackles Luther "Squabby" Parker and Thomas Hopkins, guards Grover Stewart and Henry Lavender, center Cecil Stiles, and, most importantly, halfback John P. Cox. The new coach must have hoped for more than he saw in the twenty-eight boys who showed up, because he published a plea in the school paper the following week for all the school's boys to try out for the team. Freshmen Charles Bassler from Temple, Osborn, and Oscar Golson emerged in fall drills as depth-chart movers. Coach Stewart tweaked his lineup repeatedly, seeking the best performance from his team.

The team scheduled two scrimmages—the first with Dallas University, which backed out, and a second with Britton Training School (today it would be called a junior college) in Cisco, Texas. Fort Worth High School filled in the spot vacated by the team from Dallas, and held the college boys to 19 points, scoring 0. The Britton Training School held them to 16. (The yearbook photo shows 19-0). Golson scored both TCU touchdowns.

The team played for more than good feelings: a local firm that operated a shoe store publically announced that it would give a silver trophy to the winner of the Thanksgiving game between TCU and Polytechnic. Alumnus and former football player Grantland Anderson was part owner

Bryant F. "Bun" Ware,
captain of the 1912 team.

of the business, and fully expected the Horned Frogs to win the prize.

As expected, the season opened in Austin with a loss—the fifth consecutive loss for the Horned Frogs. But 30-10 was a more respectable loss than many other teams suffered at the hands of the Longhorns. In the second quarter, John P. Cox scored at the end of a long drive, only to see the points taken away because of a penalty. TCU got another stab at a touchdown late in the game when Charlie Walton scampered sixty-five yards for six points; this time the referees did not take them away.

The Frogs' fortunes finally turned in Georgetown the following week, against Southwestern. The Pirates were one of Texas's most successful college teams in preceding years. Coach Stewart tried another pair of starting ends in Blue Rattan and Ed Stewart. The black and gold team had no answer for John P. Cox's running (he scored three touchdowns) or TCU's defense (Southwestern never crossed TCU's forty-yard line). TCU won, 20–0. At that point, the Frogs' longest unbeaten streak had been seven games, at the height of E. J. Hyde's tutelage in 1906–07. The victory over Southwestern began a twelve-game streak of wins and ties that the Frogs wouldn't exceed for another thirteen years.

Coach Stewart outcoached his rival at Baylor, again tweaking the lineup before the game. Instead of William Rattan at right end, Coach started Jack Stratton; Bugs Thannish and Joe McCullum played at right halfback instead of Charlie Walton, who moved to backup quarterback. The coach still hadn't found the best lineup until Baylor opened the game with nine carries for forty-five yards, and Stewart replaced the starting left guard (Overton) with Grover Stewart. The substitution stiffened TCU's defense, and Baylor's offense stalled. The Frogs used further substitutions sparingly, while Baylor kept cycling players in and out, unable to find a combination that could work any success against TCU.

The game was scoreless going into the second quarter, despite Jack Stratton carrying the ball into Baylor's end zone in the first quarter. He had picked up an incomplete pass, and being unsure whether or not the ball touched the ground, ran it in, but the score was disallowed. Stratton picked off a Baylor pass (before it touched the ground) to open the second quarter. The play of the game came a few drives later when Walton picked off another Baylor pass and ran it fifty yards for a score. TCU missed the point after, and went into halftime only six points ahead. John P. Cox tallied another fifty-yard run returning the opening kickoff at the second half. The drive stalled, and after the teams traded a few punts, Cox scored the second touchdown of the game on a twenty-five-yard run. Cox also kicked in the point after. By the fourth quarter, TCU players—especially John P. Cox—couldn't buy bad luck. When Cox attempted a long pass to Bussey that was deflected by Baylor, TCU's Walton made a headlong dive at Baylor's five-yard line and came up with the ball before it hit the ground. Two plays later, Cox ran it in himself for the game's final touchdown. TCU beat Baylor 22–0, its first win against its rival since it moved to Fort Worth.

The most anticipated matchup of the season came the next week against Austin College. Three thousand spectators were on hand to watch TCU, playing without Bun Ware, take on the team from Sherman. Ware was missed when twice in the first half the Frog defense allowed Austin College within three yards of the goal. But each time the Frogs rose up and took possession on downs. The teams replayed the act almost without variation in the third quarter, TCU again holding Austin College right at the goal line for no score. Blue Rattan and John P. Cox played alternately at quarterback; both had gains on the ground and in the air. Cox scored the only points of the game in the second quarter—both the touchdown and the point after. The Frogs held on to win the nail-biter, 7–0.

Two easy games came next: a short trip to Polytechnic, to end October, a game TCU won 33–3, and a romp with Howard Payne, which TCU won by over fifty points. Poly's coach frankly acknowledged that the better team had won the game, but vowed that "by Thanksgiving I will have a team that will make the Christians play ball."[60] Facing Trinity in Waxahachie the next week, for the first time since the season opener TCU found itself trailing—the score standing 7–2 early in the first quarter. The Frogs shook off the reversal, however, and finished 48–13, being held on downs only once. Charles Bassler, John P. Cox, and Blue Rattan

John P. Cox, halfback, around 1911.

stood out on offense, Grover Stewart on defense.

Despite the school's best efforts to talk up Polytechnic for the Thanksgiving game, the event felt anticlimactic compared to previous emotional Turkey Day bouts with Baylor. Only "hundreds" of fans attended, and they saw the Frogs take a three-score lead into the fourth quarter before Polytechnic managed to score on a short field. Contemporary records do not say whether or not Poly "made the Christians play ball" to win their first conference championship.

TCU's seven wins in 1912 were its most ever in a single season. Referee M. L. Massingill gave first team all-state lauds to Bun Ware (left guard), Blue Rattan (left end), John P. Cox (fullback), and second team to Charles Bassler (left halfback). Coach Stewart went to Tennessee in an attempt to convince all-state players from that state to play a game against all-state players from Texas, in Fort Worth. His idea of a postseason exhibition would take root a decade later.

TCU expected most of the team's better players to return in 1913,

C. T. "Blue" Rattan, team captain, 1913.

including newly elected captain Blue Rattan, and anticipated continued success when the dam burst. The problem centered on C. C. Campbell, a shortstop who transferred to TCU and quickly became captain of the baseball team, which Stewart coached. Campbell's power hitting drove the Frogs' sandlot success in 1912, but the wins aroused the scrutiny of rival fans. One such fan noticed Campbell in a photo of the 1911 team he played on. His appearance at TCU in 1912—under his twin brother's name—was illegal. Coach Stewart knew of the plot, which worsened the crime in the eyes of the conference officials.

TCU maintained that Campbell had legally enrolled and played, and only gave a false name to a newspaperman. But to whomever it was given, the false statement broke the rules. Campbell disappeared from box scores by April 24; a professor named Nance took over the coaching duties. Campbell and Stewart left the school, and took its spirit with them. Denial proliferated. "There is something wrong," intoned the *Skiff* that day. "[J]ust exactly what this fault is remains a problem for the best to work on."[61]

TCU maintained its innocence. Speakers at the postseason banquet for the baseball team made every effort to avoid mention of the scandal. Athletic committee members and alumni rose to speak, and extolled the team and the school's clean athletics. One alumnus and booster went so

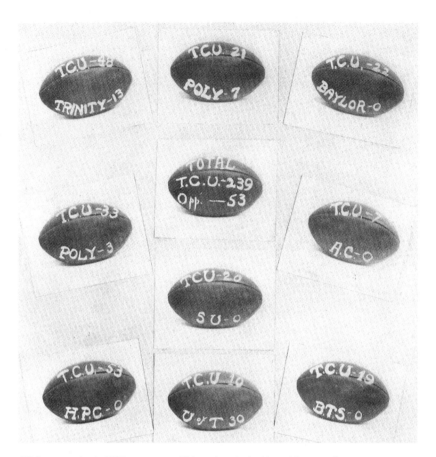

TCU's seven wins in 1912 were a team high, and made the Horned Frogs conference champions for the first time. (The BTS win was a scrimmage.)

far as to say clean athletics was the only kind TCU had ever played.[62] Some students and even some faculty members tried to convince the TIAA to be merciful and not punish their school. Their efforts produced the opposite result, and on May 9 the TIAA expelled TCU from the conference and barred the coach for two years. TCU in turn expelled C. C. Campbell and dismissed the coach, both of whom had already departed the school.

Some TCU fans thought the Horned Frogs were punished more than other schools that had committed similar infractions. Ironically, the president of the TIAA during the investigation and the punishment was Dr. C. C. Gumm, of Polytechnic College. He joined the TCU faculty, amid some unpopularity, in 1915, after Polytechnic College closed (or, in theory, merged with SMU). TCU appointed a trio of professors to lead the athletic department, including C. I. Alexander, who had payed on TCU's first football team. Thirty years later Colby Hall wrote that Stewart and Campbell recovered their reputations. His optimism is undercut, however, by his refusal to give their names.

1913

The scandal sucked the wind—which had become considerable—out of TCU's sails. TCU could not even compete to extend its reign as champion of the TIAA. The *Skiff* moaned that football practices were not being observed by the students: "There are students in school who do not even know that we have a team."[63] But indeed there was a team, led by Professor Frederick M. Cahoon, coaching without extra pay, and aided by some players—Bun Ware (who did not play) and Luke Ray (who did).

Coach Cahoon might be the most colorful character in TCU's early era. He hailed from Temple, and had coached one of TCU's championship baseball teams a few years earlier. Cahoon and his glamorous wife, Helen Fouts Cahoon, had mildly successful musical careers in New York (Mr. Cahoon on the violin, Mrs. Cahoon singing) before returning to TCU as music professors. Mrs. Cahoon taught voice at TCU. Her husband was more versatile.

In this second career at TCU, Cahoon served as director of the orchestra and glee club, directed a travelling vocal quartet (they went as far as Denver), and was university band director, playing tuba himself. He was an automobile enthusiast, an expert tennis player, and coached the football and basketball teams when required, usually as an assistant. Eventually he led the entire athletic department. His and Mrs. Cahoon's sudden resignations and removal from TCU late in the fall semester of 1919 shocked the students, and ended one of the most colorful careers of any TCU professor or coach in its long history. The Cahoons continued to entertain TCU and Fort Worth society, despite their separation from the school.

Cahoon did more than merely hold the program together during the school's year without a conference. His 1913 team performed admirably, given the circumstances. The continuity and tutelage Cahoon provided as an assistant coach through the turbulence of the war years is one of the great and forgotten individual contributions to TCU football.

The football team looked different in 1913. It played in new uniforms, and played without John P. Cox. Allan Freeman nearly sat out a year with Cox, but was persuaded to rejoin the team. Instead of the familiar matches with Baylor, Trinity, Austin College, Southwestern, and the other TIAA schools, TCU lined up a motley schedule primarily of high school

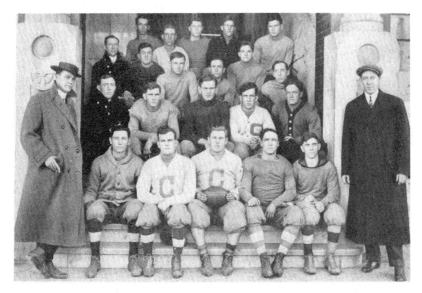

The 1913 squad. Frederick M.Cahoon stands at left, in the greatcoat.

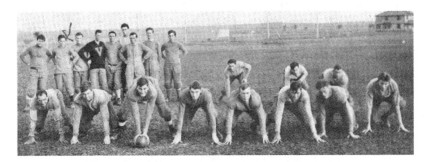

Lineup, 1913. The team appears here in an unusual formation, apparently with some linemen moved from the right to left, and without a quarterback.

and YMCA teams, and played football nonetheless.

The opener in Weatherford against a high school team was a defensive slugfest. Revealingly, neither team scored. TCU held the younger boys to zero first downs. Joe McNamara intercepted all of Weatherford's attempts to pass. But playing a high school team only to a tie signaled that the reigning TIAA champion was a shell of its former self.

Shell or not, the Horned Frogs still outlasted the local YMCA team. The YMCA team did get two first downs, and scored on an eighty-yard fumble recovery. TCU's McCowan didn't play, and in his place Alvin Street

Ends, 1913. Left to right: Jack Stratton, [unidentified], W. Luther Parker, Ed Stewart.

quarterbacked the team and Luther "Squabby" Parker passed with success from his fullback position. Street tallied one sixty-yard run in the first half; Joe McNamara took one of Parker's passes twenty yards for a score. The YMCA players called for curtains shortly before the fourth quarter, and the game was called with TCU ahead 32–6.

Dallas University came to Fort Worth next, in another defensive game that was scoreless until the last few minutes, when at last the Dallas team got a successful line plunge at the goal line, and a few plays later kicked a field goal to beat TCU 3–0.

The tenor of the season was reflected in the betting line for TCU's rematch with Howard Payne in Brownwood. The home team had narrowly missed beating Baylor the week before, and sought revenge against TCU for their humbling fifty-three point loss at the Horned Frogs' hands in 1912. The money favored Horward Payne, but three times Howard Payne drove to the Horned Frogs' one-yard line, and three times TCU rose up and took back possession on downs. The game's only score came on a pick-six by TCU end Cooper in the closing minutes; Reeder made the extra point after, and TCU won 7–0.

A pick-six again gave TCU the first points in a game the following week against the Fort Worth YMCA, shortly into the third quarter. Center

On the gridiron, 1913.

Crawford Reeder had success stopping runners behind the line, and the game ended 14–0. Reeder was the son of an Amarillo lawyer who came to TCU to study law. He won his class award in the literary society twice, and returned to Amarillo as a partner in his father's practice after his career at TCU.

TCU travelled to Greenville next, defeating Burleson College 25–0, and eating well with their hosts after the game. The score would have been even more lopsided, but the Frogs fumbled away multiple runs that likely would have ended in points. Reeder again camped out in the opponent's backfield, tallying multiple tackles for loss.

The season ended with a narrow loss to Dallas University. Much like the game against Howard Payne, the match went scoreless for most of the game. Both teams missed field goals and failed to capitalize on interceptions. The Catholics finally broke the logjam when it recovered a TCU fumble at its own three-yard line, and scored the game's only points shortly thereafter.

The season's winning record went some way to obscuring the pall under which the year had begun. Center Reeder was elected captain for 1914, and the team celebrated Professor Cahoon's effort to salvage the program at a dinner at his home. Cahoon stayed on as an assistant coach.

1914

When Old TCU's team falls in line,
We're going to win again another time
For Varsity we'll yell, yell, yell,
For the foot ball team we love so well, oh well,
We're going to fight, fight, fight for every score,
Circle ends and then we'll win some more.
And we'll roll Old Baylor in the sod (we said the sod—)
Roll—Roll—ROLL!

—TCU Varsity Song

In a way, the 1914 season was a success before it began. The TIAA reinstated TCU, allowing it to schedule football games with other members. The school hired Polytechnic's football coach, S. A. Boles, who had learned the sport at Vanderbilt. John P. Cox was back in action after sitting out the 1913 season. Cox also led a new campus Sunday school. Ben Gantt, Alvin Street, Ray Fox, Joe McNamara, and Crawford Reeder also returned. The players donned uniforms with a capital "C" on the front.

New players came with acclaim. Four from Fort Worth High School had just won the state championship: end Howard Vaughn, tackle Jesse Martin, Garth, and Phillips. Otis "Judge" Ramsey, who came with Coach Boles from Poly along with Ronald Garrett, Evans, and Clyde Miller, challenged Griffin at quarterback. The players from Poly could play immediately because their former team had disbanded.

Coaches Boles and Cahoon held training camp in Venus, Texas, southeast of Fort Worth. After practices, the boys played in a nearby lake. The city housed the sunburned team in the local high school. The city's hopes to host the Frogs' camp annually remained unfulfilled.

TCU scrimmaged with North Texas State Normal College, today called University of North Texas, a week prior to the opening game. The Horned Frogs passed brilliantly, and won 40–0. TCU looked like world-beaters.

Those offensive fireworks sputtered in the season opener on a Friday in Georgetown against Southwestern. TCU drew the first blood of the game when it drove to the Methodists' five-yard line, turned the ball over on

Left to right: "Squabby" Parker, Crawford Reeder, Alvin Street.

downs, and then downed the Southwestern ball carrier in the end zone for a safety. In the second quarter, John P. Cox threw a touchdown to Joe McNamara, and kicked the extra point to increase the lead to nine. TCU still led 9–3 into the fourth quarter, but after holding Southwestern on downs at the TCU fifteen-yard line, the Frogs punted to the forty-five only to let the returner score. TCU failed to answer, and lost the game by one point.

After a half-day holiday for students to attend the Stock Show, the Frogs played the Miners from the Oklahoma School of the Mines. It being TCU's second game but only the Oklahomans' first, the TCU crowd expected victory and got a resounding one. The Frogs started hot, scoring on its first drive, which included a sensational weaving forty-yard run by John P. Cox, and a successful fake punt, forward pass, and five-yard plunge near the goal line by Jude Bivins for the game's first points. Bivins repeated the act in the second quarter for the second score, and John "Cal" Nelson would have made a third touchdown before halftime, but he let go of the ball in the end zone for a Miner touchback. (The old rule that a player must down the ball in the end zone to score was still in force.) Judge Ramsey received the final touchdown on a pass from Wilbur Brown in the third quarter. The Miners threatened to score in the fourth, but their drive stalled, and their kicker missed the field goal that would have prevented the shutout. TCU won 20–0.

Texas A&M completely turned the tables on TCU in College Station the next week. Texas A&M had a talent and schematic advantage, playing heavier men in a "revolving wedge" formation. The newspapers, calling it

Jude Bivins, 1914.

a variation on a "Pennsylvania Tandem" formation, described it as three men in the backfield blocking for one man who acts "as a pivot."[64] A&M scored three touchdowns in each half of the game with the play. Judge Ramsey and John P. Cox drew applause from the home crowd for interceptions and brave running, respectively. The Horned Frogs threatened to score in the fourth, netting fifty yards on three passes, but the Aggies intercepted the fourth, and with it sealed the shutout 40-0.

The following week, Coach Boles took eighteen players to Houston to face the Rice Owls, for Rice's first battle with TCU on the gridiron. The Rice Institute was only a couple of years old, and had begun football in the TIAA in 1913. Both teams played a soaked, muddy, fumble-filled, and scoreless game.

Baylor was 1–3–1 heading into its rivalry game with TCU. It had suffered horrendous blowouts at the hands of University of Texas and Oklahoma A&M. Jude Bivins, who did not make the trip to Houston, travelled to Waco; his return to left guard was not enough to spur the Frogs to victory. Crawford Reeder at center got hurt in the first quarter, but was ably replaced by Ben Gantt.

While TCU ran the ball up the middle better than Baylor, the Bears passed better than the Frogs—including double and triple passing—and ran better end-arounds. In the first quarter, Baylor drove to TCU's four, and on third and four won another set of downs when TCU moved offsides; Baylor scored on third and two. Baylor threatened again in the second quarter, driving to TCU's fifteen-yard line, but fumbled the ball to Jesse

Martin, who returned the ball eighty-five yards for a score. The game went aerial thereafter; the remaining four touchdowns of the game—three for Baylor, one for TCU—were all on pass plays, the last for Baylor on a fifty-yard toss and score. One ground play stood out, however, in the third quarter, when Baylor's star player Fouts got loose for seventy yards. Baylor won 28–14.

Not all Horned Frogs left Waco losers, however. The matron of a Baylor dorm discovered a TCU student and a "fair [Baylor] coed making love at an old well near the university," and punished all of the Baylor girls with "a severe curtain lecture about holding clandestine meetings with the boys at the well to court."[65]

Perhaps spurred to vigor by their classmate's conquest, the Horned Frogs recovered their moxie in Fort Worth the following week and bested the Austin College Kangaroos. The 13–0 win was littered with punts. John P. Cox again shone brightly for the Frogs, especially in passing.

The next weekend featured a doubleheader, almost. The Horned Frogs traveled to Brownwood to play both of the local teams, Daniel Baker on Saturday, and Howard Payne on Monday. Daniel Baker upset the Frogs, 33–0. John P. Cox's punting (he averaged over forty yards per boot) was the only bright spot for TCU.

The Frogs juggled the lineup for their Monday match against Howard Payne. The only starters who played both games at the same position were the center Crawford Reeder and right tackle Ewell McKnight. Judge Ramsay, Wallace, Jesse Martin, Wilbur Brown, and John P. Cox started at different positions, and the changes worked wonders. Neither team scored until the fourth quarter, but TCU was otherwise considerably more productive, passing successfully and converting third downs. Cox jump-started the Frogs' offense with a fifty-yard rush, followed by a pass to Nash that set up the first score of the game. TCU drove for its second score on its next possession. Cox made both points after; the game ended 14–0.

A sharp cold front swept over North Texas on Thanksgiving, chilling the students, alumni, and fans who had come into town from as far as Brownwood to see the game with Trinity. The Tigers' manager contacted Dr. Gumm before the game and asked for a postponement on account of the rainy, cold weather. Dr. Gumm agreed, fearing the players would develop pneumonia if the game went ahead as scheduled. Most high schools also postponed or cancelled their Thanksgiving games, although the TCU-Trinity game was the only college match in the state that was postponed.

When the teams finally suited up on Monday, Trinity jumped out to a 6–0 lead when, on its first possession, a TCU player jumped offsides, prompting a whistle. The Trinity player with the ball kept running all the way to the end zone, and by the rules of the day, was given the choice

FOOTBALL

Board of
Strategy

COACH BOLES
CAPTAIN REEDER
COACH CAHOON

The 1914 "Board of Strategy": left to right Coach Boles, Captain Crawford Reeder, Coach Cahoon.

of taking the penalty yardage or the yardage gained on the play—and the points. After that initial outburst, the game settled into a defensive slugfest. TCU failed to score from within Trinity's five-yard line on no less than six different drives. John P. Cox had many long runs, but the Trinity defense kept TCU out of the end zone all but once in the third quarter. The game finished a tie.

Trinity liked what they saw in the TCU team, and hired away Coach Boles for its 1915 season. John P. Cox was unanimously elected captain of the 1915 TCU team, and made an all-state team selected by a committee of referees. End Ralph "Gish" Martin was later called TCU's best all-around player in 1914, even though he did not even earn a letter that year.

1915

Optimism buoyed TCU in 1915. It expected to enroll one thousand students for the first time. It also opened a two-year law program, the Brite College of the Bible, and began a focus on its business college. Students paid a ten-dollar fee in the fall for season tickets to all of the football games and oratorical contests.

TCU hired Ewing Young Freeland to coach the team and to proctor the Clark Hall dorm. Alum Milton Daniel and the steadiest Horned Frog,

Coach Cahoon, assisted Coach Freeland.

E. Y. Freeland was not afraid to have his team throw the ball around; his was the first Horned Frog squad to depend on the pass to move the ball. It worked against all but three teams in 1915: Texas, Rice, and Baylor.

Milton Daniel was more influential than TCU assistant coaches traditionally had been. A 1912 TCU graduate, he had gone on to earn a law degree in Austin, where he starred again on a football team—this time for UT. He had returned to his alma mater to teach law. During the 1915 season he made a notable speech to a gathering of Dallas alumni after the Austin College game, and motivated TCU's trustees to construct an athletic field on campus. The field and gymnasium were initially projected to cost $10,000, and were to include a "spacious grandstand . . . gridiron, baseball diamond, track, and basketball courts."[66] The school hoped that the new facilities would attract high school activities, complement athletic recruiting, and serve to facilitate the new physical education requirements for all students. Not surprisingly, the projected cost of the facilities more than doubled within a year, but the school did not flinch. Late in 1916, when the administration announced at a daily chapel that it was committing $25,000 to the project from a large-scale fundraising campaign, the students cheered for three minutes.

Freeland held preseason camp for two weeks at Six Mile Dam, located a few miles west of campus. The coach discouraged his players from talking about what they would do; instead they should let their actions do the talking. He gave the team the motto, "First the deeds, then the glory." When John P. Cox was telling the *Skiff* about this plan, the coach tapped Cox on the shoulder and reminded him, "Now you're talking. We are going to do something first."[67]

Starting ends Gish Martin, Joe McNamara, and Howard "Shorty" Vaughn, guard Raymond Fox, fullbacks John P. Cox and John "Cal" Nelson all returned, as did starter Otis "Judge" Ramsey. Backup guards Abe Greines and W. B. Higgins expected to make the first team. Two transfers, John Lattimore, a two-hundred-pound transfer from Baylor who was studying at TCU's medical school, and Frank "Peanuts" McKee, the star quarterback from Bryant's Training School, hoped to make the team. Neither made the trip to Austin at the beginning of the season.

Freshmen included Eddie Stangl, Denton "Froggie" Hawes, and Loudon Sewell, from local high schools. Coach Freeland held a scrimmage against North Side High School the week prior to the game in Austin; TCU only scored once, but shut out the high schoolers.

The coaches kept competition for spots on the varsity squad open until the first game, against the University of Texas. The Longhorns had returned most of their undefeated 1914 team, and TCU hardly registered in Austin, being outweighed by about twenty pounds a man and losing

Guard Raymond Fox, 1914.

by 72 points. TCU gave up 547 yards in end runs alone, but held UT's quarterback, Littlefield, to six completions in nineteen attempts.

John P. Cox was ill and did not play the Frogs' first game against new SMU. It hardly mattered, however, because SMU, playing in its first year, had no experienced players. The only players who had experience playing college ball were transfers, and thus ineligible for a season. These ineligible players practiced as scrubs against the eligible but inexperienced players—with predictable results. SMU's newspaper, the *Campus*, spilled quite a bit of ink trying to convince its readers that their team was up to the challenge, and trying to coax students to travel and cheer on the freshmen—but only fifteen fans from Dallas made the trip. They saw an inept offense fumble repeatedly while attempting to pass the ball. TCU recovered most of the fumbles, and scored most of its points in the first half. By the final whistle the score was 43–0. SMU went 2–5 in 1915, scoring only three touchdowns all season.

The third game of the year, one of several held during the state fair in Dallas, was a lopsided Tuesday afternoon victory for the Frogs on a muddy Fair Park field against Austin College. "Peppery Jo" Edens had taken over passing and kicking extra points. TCU outgained the Kangaroos from Sherman on the ground (182 to 154 yards), in the air (264 to 17), and on punts (41 yards in six attempts to 28 yards in twelve attempts). Judge Ramsey was the star, both on end runs (he had three over twenty yards) and punt returns.

Late in the Austin College game, Edens passed forty-five yards in the air to Howard Vaughn, who ran with the ball the remaining forty yards to the end zone. John P. Cox got in on the passing game as well—passing to Edens and catching a couple himself. Freshman Eddie Stangl was punting, and well. Two punts against the Kangaroos went for fifty yards. The final score was 28–0.

TCU played a very close game against Texas A&M on Friday of the next week. Fans expected a heavy loss. When TCU slowed the Farmers' ground attack, A&M tried to move the ball primarily by passing, and failed. TCU had much the same dilemma—it couldn't rush the ball. But it did better in the air, where Edens's passes connected repeatedly with Cooper and Vaughn. The Horned Frogs nearly kept A&M off the board in the first quarter, holding the Farmers out of the end zone for a series of three straight rushes at the goal line. But on the fourth attempt A&M's Kendricks bucked "barely" over the line to put the Farmers in the lead. Cal Nelson narrowed the lead to four with a field goal in the second quarter, and neither team scored again until the fourth. A&M returned to the ground game and scored another touchdown.

Eddie Stangl's fifty-five-yard pick-six, when the Frogs were down ten points, headlined the match. As the *Star-Telegram* described it, "[W]ith less than two minutes to play in the final quarter the TCU tackle speared one of [A&M's] passes after it had been blocked by Vaughn and cleverly evading two A&M tacklers planted the oval behind the Farmers' goal." [68] The near upset prompted a sharp rise in enthusiasm for the team in Fort Worth. The student fan club doubled its numbers. Some players may have gotten carried away in the exuberance. An indirect remonstrance of an unnamed football player appeared in that week's *Skiff*, flattering him with the knowledge that his personal conduct was generally known and judged by the student body, and warning him that he was expected to play clean on and off the field.

The Horned Frogs rode the H&TC Southland train for Rice in Houston, healthier than they had been all season. TCU left its ground game in Fort Worth, as the Frogs could only gain ten rushing yards in Houston, depending almost entirely on the forward pass to convert on third downs. The unbalanced attack netted only three points in Houston, and TCU lost by thirty.

TCU was already looking ahead to the Thanksgiving game with Baylor when it met Trinity at Waxahachie in early November. But anti-Baylor feelings did not distract the Frogs so much that they could not beat the Tigers. John P. Cox and "Peppery Joe" Edens took turns passing; the Frogs scored once in each quarter (twice in the fourth, but for a holding penalty) and won 25–0. TCU also shut out Southwestern in Fort Worth, 21–0. The head lineman told the writer for the *Skiff* that Ramsey, in his opinion, was the best punt returner in Texas. [69] The shutout streak continued—

in the inverse—when Oklahoma A&M brought the traditional run-heavy game to Fort Worth and won the first game on a newly christened YMCA Field, 13–0. The mayor of Fort Worth kicked the game ball, about ten yards, to open play, although the officials had an A&M player re-kick to begin the actual game. The difference in the two teams' styles of play could not have been starker. Oklahoma A&M did not even attempt a forward pass, and gained 218 yards by line plunges, frequently in a tackle-around-tackle play that stymied TCU's defense. TCU could only manage twenty-one yards plunging up the middle, but gained 205 in the air. Those aerial yards came on only ten completed passes, however—a frustrating game for the Frogs.

At last the day came for the Thanksgiving game with Baylor. Students could take a train round-trip for $1.25. The largest crowd in "many moons" watched the game at Carroll Field. On the line for Baylor was its shutout streak against other Texas teams, but TCU rode south to Waco hoping to win a stake in the TIAA title. What it got instead was one of the most lopsided games in the rivalry's lengthening history. Perhaps Baylor had scouted the Frogs' vulnerability to line plunges; certainly the Bears' backfield was one of its best ever, featuring Theron Fouts, Lucian Roach, and Howard Wilson.

The wind hampered "Peppery Joe" Edens's passing. The Bears scored on short drives featuring long runs, and long drives of short runs. Baylor was up 20-0 before TCU had any success at all. Gish Martin intercepted a Baylor pass to start a TCU drive that covered forty-eight yards (thirty-five on a long run by Edens) before it was stalled by incomplete passes. Then Baylor blocked TCU's punt. Nothing was going TCU's way—even Baylor's halftime snake dance was better than TCU's. By game's end, the score was 51-0. The locals were not impressed with John P. Cox, but thought Judge Ramsey was as good as advertised.

It turned out, however, that the Bears were not playing fair. Some of their players were ineligible, and the game result was thrown out by the TIAA once this came to light—although the conference did not think the offense so great as to oust Baylor from the conference for an entire year.

Ralph "Gish" Martin, a law student, was elected captain of the next season's squad at a soiree held for the team at Coach Cahoon's home. The only dissenting vote was Martin's own.

1916

Even with a new Fort Worth-Dallas rivalry with SMU in the making, it was TCU's loss to Baylor in 1915 that motivated the 1916 team. The *Skiff* boasted that TCU's improved team in 1916 would promise "old Baylor a 'bloody battle' next Thanksgiving."[70]

TCU promoted Milton Daniel in 1916 to head coach, athletic director, and track coach. Daniel kept Cahoon as his assistant coach, and kept Coach Freeland's ethic of letting deeds do the speaking for the team as well. He also made a habit of avoiding scheduling Texas (his other alma mater) and Texas A&M. The state schools obliged, perhaps wishing to distance themselves from a school playing in a conference (TIAA) that lacked the prestige of the new and rising Southwest Conference.

In 1916 Coach Daniel and captain Gish Martin hoped that incoming players would bolster the line and backfield and help improve the Frogs' rushing attack against good defenses. Their hopes centered on seven incoming freshmen from Vernon, recruited by Coach Daniel on a trip up US 287 to Denver that also netted halfback "Keggy" Calvert from Amarillo. "Bun" Ware and Cecil Stiles, from the 1912 team, were back in school and on the team again. Ultimately only two from Vernon matriculated and joined the team, halfbacks Bill Berry and Liles. Calvert started at fullback for the team all season. A pair of two-sport standouts for the Horned Frogs enrolled in '16—center Astyanax Douglass and halfback Leo "Dutch" Meyer. As students, they would make names for themselves in baseball as much as (if not more than) they did in football.

During training camp, held at Camp Tyra at Lake Worth, Gish Martin injured his knee. Then Ox Kornegay broke his hip in the team's

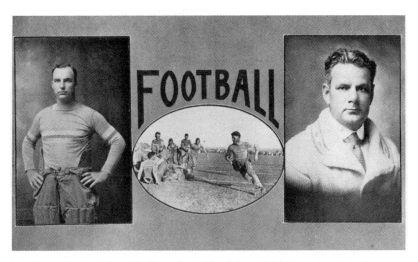

Coach Milton Daniel (left) and Assistant Coach M. F. Cahoon (right). The center photo shows the first touchdown of the Thanksgiving 1916 game against Baylor. From the 1917 yearbook.

scrimmage against North Side High School. By the season opener, Howard Vaughn and Cal Nelson also were out with injuries. Bill Berry carried the Frogs' hopes for the class of Vernon players by himself, and proved as good as advertised.

The season started well against Austin College with good cheering from the crowd, and lots to cheer for. After stopping a long Kangaroos drive on downs at TCU's eight-yard line, Pug Calvert plunged for two yards, and then Edens ran the remaining ninety through the entire Austin College team for the game's first score. Austin College's next drive stalled, and TCU blocked the punt and took over at the Kangaroos' thirteen-yard line. Calvert fumbled, but TCU recovered, and after Bill Berry recovered the yardage, Calvert carried the ball three times in succession for a score.

Austin College's only points, and the only points in the middle quarters of the game, came when Dutch Meyer muffed a punt in the end zone and was downed for a safety. Bill Berry scored a thirty-five-yard touchdown in the third quarter, but it was called back because the referee did not blow his whistle during a substitution. The Frogs returned to the line of scrimmage and drove methodically toward Austin College's end zone, but did not score. TCU intercepted a pass to end the Kangaroos' next drive, and Calvert scored the fourth and final TCU touchdown of the game shortly after. TCU finished 28–2.

The 1916 team, as pictured in the 1917 yearbook. Left to right: Martin, tackle, 1916 captain; Tudor, Manager; Nelson, halfback; Greines, guard; Vaughn, end; Stangl, end.

The 1916 team. Left to right: Edens, quarterback; Kornegay, tackle; Calvert, fullback; "Willie," tackle; Douglass, center; Broadley, guard.

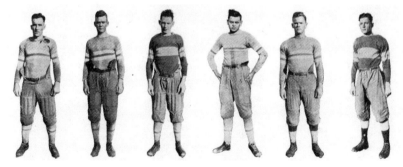

The 1916 team. Left to right: Berry, halfback; Ogilvie, end; Bradford, center; Hawes, tackle; Elliott, end; Meyers, halfback.

In the weeks between the opener and the trip to Dallas for the SMU game, Gish Martin had appendicitis, requiring surgery. He received a train of visitors and many flowers in the hospital, and wished the team and its new captain—John "Cal" Nelson—well.

TCU exceeded its forty-three-point margin of victory over SMU from 1915 in the schools' second meeting in 1916, beating the Dallasites in Fair Park by forty-five points. SMU scored on its first possession, but did not score again. Joe Edens answered with a sixty-three- (or fifty-three-) yard scoring run on TCU's first possession, and the rout was on. Edens threw three touchdown passes to Eddie Stangl, and a fourth to Howard Vaughn. Stangl made seven of eight in field goal attempts. The final score was 48–3.

TCU was the underdog hosting Rice on a Friday, but played harder than the Owls from the get-go. The teams were well matched, and fought like dragons. Spectators called it the best game of football they'd seen in years. "Peppery Joe" Edens, playing with broken ribs, nearly threw a touchdown pass in the first quarter to Frank Ogilvie. TCU kept the ball in Rice territory, and scored its only touchdown in the second quarter on an aerial pass that Cal Nelson had to jump very high to bring down with his fingertips. Rice answered in the third quarter with a long drive of short end runs that finished with a thirty-five-yard scoring scamper by Brown. TCU's backfield of Bill Berry, Pug Calvert, and Dutch Meyer could gain yardage in midfield, but not at the goal lines. Nelson eventually replaced injured quarterback Edens, and then was himself injured and had to leave the game. The tilt ended in a 7–7 tie.

The injury list that had grown so long before the Rice game had been whittled down to one, "Peppery Joe" Edens, in time for the match with Trinity. Nelson and Ogilvie subbed for him, and were effective against the hapless Presbyterians. The Trinity team, who outweighed TCU slightly, held TCU for downs twice near its goal line in the first quarter, but yielded to the Horned Frogs thereafter. Astyanax Douglass, the center, snagged two interceptions. Cal Nelson threw three touchdowns to Vaughn, and ran for two himself on plunges. The game finished 35–0.

TCU took a five-game unbeaten streak to Georgetown, leaving Joe Edens and Ox Kornegay at home recovering from injuries. The star for the Southwestern Pirates, A. G. Knickerbocker, ran through TCU seemingly at will, and the Frogs, who were favored, lost 41–13.

Another double feature the next weekend in Brownwood tested the team's conditioning. Coach Daniel took Ox Kornegay but hoped not to need him for the games against Daniel Baker and Howard Payne, preferring him fully healed for the Baylor game at the close of the season. He rethought that strategy and played Kornegay and Edens on Saturday against Daniel Baker.

Daniel Baker had beaten Southwestern and Knickerbocker, which worried the Frogs. The undefeated Hillbillies were trumpeting their run for the state championship; to date they had not given up any points. TCU ended the shutout streak in the game's first quarter when Cal Nelson, Joe Edens, and Pug Calvert drove the ball near the goal. Edens connected with center Astyanax Douglass for the first score, and a few minutes later connected with end Eddie Stangl for the second. TCU added a safety in the quarter, to make it 18–0 before the second quarter. The game settled into a punting contest for two quarters, Ox Kornegay repeatedly making tackles behind Daniel Baker's line. Edens and Stangl connected in the fourth for a forty-five-yard touchdown pass for the game's final points. TCU won 23–0.

Two days later the Frogs rained down six touchdowns on the hapless Howard Payne in the first quarter—Dutch Meyer and Joe Edens each had a pair on the ground, and one each for Pug Calvert, Cal Nelson, and Eddie Stangl. The second team finished the game and won 48–7. The Frogs returned to Fort Worth to prepare for Baylor. TCU had five wins, one loss, and one tie, and was thick in the hunt for the TIAA championship. Also contending for the championship were the Baylor Bears, who boasted their best team to date (possibly their best ever). No team had scored a touchdown against Baylor in two seasons.

Hype—unlike any in TCU's history—attended this matchup: this was a "Game of the Century"[71] a couple decades before the famous 1935 tilt with SMU. Both teams had only one loss; both had mostly healed from injuries. Gish Martin returned to the field, at right guard.

Baylor fans were expected to flock to Fort Worth, making the biggest crowd ever to watch a game in Panther City. Coach Cahoon and students constructed twenty sections of wooden stands (with 150 box seats) to house the overflow. Coach Daniel worked out the team in the basement of Clark Hall when the weather turned sour. The slogan "Beat Baylor" peppered the *Skiff*, and, presumably, contemporary conversation. The *Lariat* thought the rivalry had "grown to a boiling point" with "intense dislike." [72]

Revenge for last season's drubbing had been the Frogs' goal all season; defending Theron Fouts's all-state plunging was the mission. Fouts, not quite five foot ten inches tall and 160 pounds, was the best of Baylor's three-pronged attack; halfbacks Lucian Roach, who played well despite a broken finger, and Howard Wilson were two and three. Wilson was the Bears' passer, one of the best in the state. He would not be the last Frog rival passer named Wilson.

About six thousand fans flocked to the game; the ticket sales generated so much revenue that the two schools would agree to play the next season's matchup in Fort Worth again. Both teams played jittery to open; Baylor

The 1916 team banquet.

flubbed an attempted fake kick; TCU fumbled away its first drive; Baylor's kicker, Roach, missed a field goal. He would miss all but one of the points after for Baylor. Jitters and emotions notwithstanding, only one penalty was called the entire game, against Baylor in the fourth quarter.

TCU then drove nearly sixty yards before throwing the ball away to Baylor's Wilson. Baylor drove across midfield by the end of the first quarter, which ended scoreless. Baylor opened the second with a series of line bucks that brought the ball to TCU's five-yard line. The Horned Frogs gave way to Fouts up the middle, and then, down one score, drove the field with passes and end runs. Cal Nelson tied the game. Baylor recovered with a forty-five-yard pass to Thompson, and then settled into another punishing drive on the ground. Fouts scored a second time, but Roach missed the point after. The score was 13–7 at the half, during which the students from both schools danced the snake dance, and the Baylor band played its favorite, "That Good Old Baylor Line."

In the third quarter, everything went wrong that could go wrong for the Frogs. Eddie Stangl kicked the ball out of bounds twice to open the half, giving Baylor the ball on its forty-five-yard line. Three Bear rushes later, from TCU's forty, Theron Fouts ran first up the middle, and then around end for a long touchdown. Fouts and Roach each tallied touchdowns just a few minutes later, notwithstanding a pair of tackles for loss by Abe Greines and Gish Martin that nearly stopped the Bears' offense for a while. TCU found itself down 32-7.

When Baylor relieved its starters, Pug Calvert intercepted a Baylor pass in the fourth to jumpstart TCU's offense in the fourth quarter. Cal Nelson passed twice to Bugs Edens for forty-nine yards and a score, but it was too little, too late. Nelson and Edens repeated the act, driving forty-five yards on two passes again, but Wilson intercepted a third pass, stymieing the comeback attempt. Baylor won 32-14 and rode home champions.

Despite the bitterness of consecutive losses to Baylor, the team celebrated an otherwise successful season. Van Zandt Jarvis presented the lettermen the gold football pins at the end of the semester. Four upperclassmen won all-state selections: quarterbacks Joe Edens, Cal Nelson, end and kicker Eddie Stangl, and guard Abe Greines. Stangl (who'd hit 97 percent of his point-after attempts) and Greines also were selected. Only one senior graduated off the team. Freshmen Astyanax Douglass, Lee Willie, Froggie Hawes, Frank Ogilvie, Cris Elliott, Dutch Meyer, Pug Calvert, and Bill Berry were as strong a freshman class as TCU had ever had. Gish Martin was again elected captain of a team facing very high expectations.

1917

World War I did not disrupt TCU football very noticeably until 1917, three years into the conflict. By then the various aspects of the Great War dominated the news. Casualty lists appeared daily in the papers— sometimes taking an entire page. At home the devastating Spanish influenza epidemic riveted public attention.

Until 1917, since Coach Hyde's days in Waco, the Horned Frogs had sported teams with significant contributors in their third and fourth years of play. The maturity and continuity this trend afforded was TCU football's first casualty of war. Upperclassmen joined the army and left school, and beginning in 1917, and accelerating in 1918 and '19, TCU teams would be largely staffed by underclassmen. Many other schools and football teams underwent a similar transition.

Despite the mayhem the war brought to the roster, TCU continued to win, to statewide surprise. In fact, it took an administrative crisis in 1919 to do what world war could not—stop TCU from winning football games.

TCU's high expectations from the 1916 season softened as expected returners did not enroll, but joined the army instead. Amid words from the front and admonitions to buy war bonds, *Skiff* readers learned in May that Cal Nelson and Peppery Joe Edens were no longer with the team. By September, almost all of the players on the team were underclassmen. Eddie Stangl, Abe Greines, Froggie Hawes, Gish Martin, Dutch Meyer, and Cecil Bradford returned. With such a young team, Coaches Daniel and Cahoon unexpectedly had their hands full.

Because so many of its players were relatively inexperienced, TCU

Paul Lockman, 1917.

actually was the underdog in the season opener against Meridian College, a Methodist school. The Frogs, led by three new backs (Heine Prinzing, Bryan Miller, Paul Lockman), and by returning quarterback Gish Martin, scored in the first quarter, but not in the second. After halftime, TCU fumbled a punt recovery, giving Meridian possession near the TCU goal. After a couple of penalties on TCU, Meridian had a first and goal at TCU's one-yard line. The Frogs held the Methodists out of the end zone in their first attempt to buck the ball over the line. On the second attempt, Paul Lockman forced a fumble, recovered it, and ran the rock ninety-nine yards for a score "before anyone had time to realize the change in conditions."[73] Miller scored a second touchdown, and Lockman made two field goals; the final was 20–0. Nobody seems to have objected that the head linesman, named Muse, was on the team of TCU's next opponent—the First Texas Artillery "Khakis," who no doubt scouted the Horned Frogs from the field.

Perhaps nobody minded because the soldiers from Camp Bowie were no match for the students on the gridiron. The Khakis' first drive stalled, and TCU drove in large yardage plays for the first score, a touchdown pass to Bradley. Paul Lockman missed the point after. The army team, substantially heavier than the students, bucked close to TCU's goal to end the first quarter. Shortly into the second quarter the Khakis finished the drive with a touchdown, and with the point after, took the lead. TCU scored again as time expired (there was some debate about whether or not

Heine Prinzing, 1917.

time had expired) on a twenty-yard pass to Roberts. TCU added a safety in the third, and then the game's final touchdown was off of an army fumble deep in its own territory that Lockman scooped up and ran in for a score.

The soldiers got a last laugh, however. A group of them held a drill a short distance from campus on Monday night, loud enough to disturb the students, putting the more romantic-minded ones on edge, expecting some sort of attack in revenge. Having worked some of the students into a tizzy, the soldiers completed their maneuvers and retreated into the darkness.

Before continuing their rivalry with SMU, TCU lost to Rice the following week in a 26–0 shutout. Lockman's passes to Bradley were the Frogs' bright spot on the otherwise glum day. SMU and TCU each had beaten Meridian early in the season—TCU by 20 points, SMU by 14. The betting line was about even. Quarterback Bryan Miller and left end Bradley, a freshman from Central High, were the stars. TCU capped its first possession with a thirty-yard scoring pass by Paul Lockman to Bradley. SMU nearly answered with a field goal, but missed the uprights. Bryan Miller bucked through the SMU line in the second quarter for the second score of the game. Lockman ran the ball in for the last score early in the third. Miller intercepted a would-be SMU touchdown pass from TCU's ten in the fourth quarter to seal the 21–0 victory. The officials tried their best to keep the score close, negating two TCU touchdowns

From the *Horned Frog,* 1918.

with penalties, and generally flagging the Horned Frogs with abandon. Nevertheless, the officials let TCU keep three touchdowns, and never had the chance to take one away from SMU. About one hundred SMU fans made the trip—a marked improvement over the last trip to Fort Worth.

TCU next beat Trinity in Waxahachie 20–6 before a loud contingent of cheering TCU students who skipped class to attend. Neither team could get its passing game to work well, though both tried valiantly to do so in the first half. At halftime the score was tied at six. Eventually the Horned Frogs refocused on the run, and got two scores out of the effort, both from Paul Lockman. Trinity was four yards from answering when the final whistle blew. Injuries in the Trinity game dampened the mood on campus all week. Bradley was not going to be able to start against Southwestern the following week, Lockman and Miller were playing through pain, and Roberts was out altogether. The Pirates' freshman quarterback, Lawrence, was called "the find" of the 1917 season.

Somehow Miller played, and bested his sensational counterpart. In front of him was an unusual lineup. Dutch Meyer played left end in Bradley's usual place, and Froggie Hawes played tackle in Troy Haire's typical spot. Marion Bralley moved to the backfield from center, in place of Gish Martin. Twice the patchwork lineup kept the Pirates out of TCU's end zone in goal-line stands in the first quarter. TCU scored twice early in the second quarter, on twenty-yard rushes by Paul Lockman and then by Marion Bralley. TCU scored again at the end of the third, and Southwestern scored its only points on a punt return in the fourth quarter. Bradley played quite a bit despite his injuries, running successfully against the Pirates. He received the last touchdown pass to push the score to 20–6. Coach Daniel liked his new lineup so well that he kept it for the remainder of the season.

The 141st Infantry "Sammies" were an undefeated army team that came to Fort Worth heavily favored to win. Perhaps TCU thought lightly of the Sammies, given the performance of their Khaki comrades earlier in the season. Certainly they were looking ahead to the Baylor game on Thanksgiving. In either case, the Horned Frogs got more than they could handle from the bigger soldiers. TCU threatened to score twice in the first quarter, but blew each opportunity with incomplete passes. Bryan Miller scored the Frogs' only touchdown; TCU gave up two, which the editors of the *Skiff* considered a victory, given the expectations going into the game. The 14–7 loss dropped TCU's record to 5-2, but still drew attention outside of Fort Worth. The *Houston Post* published a highly complementary editorial about the TCU team, crediting Milton Daniel with one of the best coaching jobs of the year for turning his green squad into winners on very short notice.

The Frogs' routed Austin College in Sherman the following week; Bryan Miller could run through the Kangaroos "like a greased pig," and the Horned Frogs "seemed to be able to make a touchdown at almost any time they chose."[74] Coach Daniel played every player who had made the trip in the second quarter. The final score was 59–0.

And then, after a rainy week, Baylor finally came to call. The matchup was not as highly anticipated in 1917 as it was in 1916, partly because both teams had lost a game earlier in the season, and because Baylor's all-state backfield from 1915–16 no longer included Theron Fouts and Howard Wilson. Lucian Roach was the sole holdover in Baylor's great mid-1910s backfield. Betting odds still favored the Bears, however, largely because the TCU squad was still relatively inexperienced. Before game day, Baylor described fullback Paul Lockman's performance as above average but had almost unreserved praise for quarterback Bryan Miller. Several hundred students expected to take the special train from Waco to Fort Worth for the game at $1.65 each round-trip ticket, but nobody expected attendance to match the six thousand mark that the Baylor-TCU game reached in 1916. TCU did not construct temporary stands, and about two thousand attended the game.

The first quarter gave no hint of the outburst to come. Both teams could gain on the other in the middle of the field, but neither could get yardage near the goal. In the second quarter, however, while Baylor's offense stalled, TCU overwhelmed Baylor both through the air and on the ground. TCU tallied three scores before halftime: a rush to the corner by Heine Prinzing, a touchdown pass from Paul Lockman to Dutch Meyer, and a twenty-five-yard end run by Bryan Miller, to make the score 20–0 going into halftime. Lockman broke up a Baylor pass to end Baylor's first possession of the second half, promptly drove the Frogs down the field on a fake pass, and finally ran the ball fifteen yards for a fourth score. After ending Baylor's next drive with a Roy Graves interception, TCU drove the full field, but did not score when Miller threw an incomplete pass into the end zone. Graves intercepted another Baylor pass to give TCU possession again. Miller ran the ball forty-five yards to the Baylor eight-yard line. Walker's open field tackle saved a touchdown (for a few minutes) and drew the only real cheers from the Baylor crowd. As the fourth quarter began, Miller passed to Lockman in the end zone, for the Frogs' last score of the game. The contest ended 34–0 in favor of the Frogs.

Baylor blamed its punchless performance on its lack of familiarity with TCU's balanced attack—an unlikely excuse given the consistency of TCU's offensive scheme from previous years—and on Miller's wily running. Mourning Baylor students buried a mascot bear in a coffin near TCU's athletic fields, but exhumed it in time for basketball and baseball season. Beating Baylor, though, defined the season for the Horned Frogs in 1917. Coach Daniel had golden stickpins made with "34-0" engraved on them, and gave one to each member of the team.[75] The number and quality of players returning for the 1917 season had raised expectations. Despite losing many returners to the war, TCU still met most of those expectations with inexperienced players. The war overseas raged unabated, but Frog fans again had high expectations for the coming year because of the number of returning players too young for the draft. Bryan Miller was selected all-state quarterback, and before the team retired for the year the players elected "Froggy" Hawes captain for 1918.

1918

It is difficult for twenty-first century students to imagine the degree to which America mobilized for the First World War. The apathy and occasional antiwar expressions that marked the early twenty-first-century campus during America's wars in the Middle East could hardly contrast more sharply with the early twentieth-century campus. By the fall of 1918, government regulations required that all male students age eighteen or older lead a quasi-military life while enrolled, even at a private school like TCU. The boys awoke early, followed a regimented schedule with ten hours of drill each week, and attended a three-hour military science class.

THE FOOTBALL SQUAD

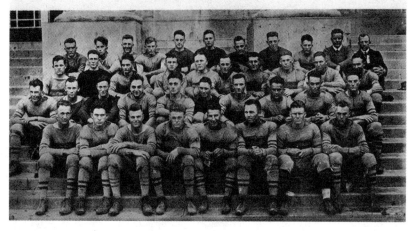

The 1918 team. Front row, left to right: Crunk, Spiller, Bradford, Haden, Miller, Chambers, Henderson, Sanders. Row 2: Haire, Singletary, E. B. Brown, Hill, Cunningham, Hale, H. Jones, W. H. Acker, Rutherford, Wages. Row 3: Moss, Irwin, Overton, Crump, Harmon, Blandford, Council, Brown, Freeman, Parks. Back row: Slay, Cross, Priest, B. Wingo, D'Moose, H. Martin, Easley, Owens, Stovall; Coaches Cahoon and Tipton.

The traditional cheers and yells were replaced by proper martial cheers and yells designed to instill the spirit of army and navy life in the college boys.

The first Horned Frog that expected to return to TCU in the fall, despite joining the army after the 1917 season, was head coach Milton Daniel. He joined the Aviation Corps as a radio telegraphy instructor (studying as he went, to stay ahead of his pupils) during Christmas break. That same break, a couple of privates in Fort Worth helped themselves to Coach Cahoon's car, getting as far as Travis County before being discovered and jailed. Cahoon got the car back, along with the added responsibilities of leading the athletic department and coaching the basketball team. Daniel hoped to be able to schedule a long furlough in the fall and retake the reins of the football team. His plan did not pan out, however, and Fred Cahoon hired E. M. Tipton to lead the team. Cahoon stayed on as an assistant coach.

The second anticipated returner to join the army was team captain Froggie Hawes. In his place, returning all-state quarterback Bryan Miller served as team captain. Dutch Meyer also missed the year while away in the army.

Coach Tipton was a hands-on kind of teacher. He broke up a fight between a writer for the *Skiff* and a visitor on the sideline during a

All-state quarterback Bryan Miller, 1918.

game. The writer—having landed a few punches of his own to end the altercation—attested to the sufficiency of the coach's fine right arm. Tipton used a long-term goal to motivate his team: beating Baylor. He devised plays especially for the Baylor game, and tried to imbue his team with the idea of killing the Baylor bear.

TCU battled the flu as much as it battled Longhorns at the opening of the season. Paul Lockman, along with new starters Red Spiller and Dave Singletary, missed the hot afternoon game entirely; Troy Haire broke an ankle in the first five minutes. TCU was, on average, light—even by TCU standards—weighing only 162 pounds per man. The freshman-heavy Frogs (all but four were playing their first collegiate game) held UT to a scoreless tie in the first half. They couldn't keep up the intensity for sixty minutes, however, and yielded three scores in the second half. The 19–0 loss was a better showing than expected, however—especially for such a shoestring team.

Carruthers Field was an aviation camp with several all-Americans and all-Western players who were now in the army. They outweighed the Frogs by thirty-five pounds a man, and not surprisingly had success on the ground against the Frogs in the first half, scoring once and shutting out TCU. But the Frogs had more fight in them, and made a game of it in the

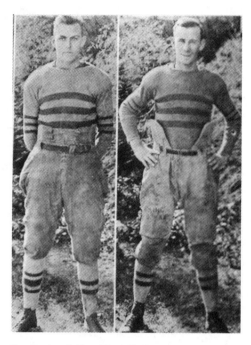

Ikey Sanders (left) and Dave Singletary.

second half. Driving to the Carruthers four-yard line, on a TCU second down the referee yelled, "Fourth down!" and when TCU did not gain ten yards, mistakenly gave the ball to Carruthers. Miller tossed a scoring pass to Lalla in the second half, but Lalla missed the point after. TCU lost 7–6.

After defeating Southwestern the next week by a score of 14–6, SMU claimed its first victory against TCU the following week in a game that was never played. TCU's players, riding in an open truck seven miles to the school in a windy, cold rain, got stuck in mud only half a mile from SMU. Coach Rix, who TCU claimed could see the freezing Horned Frog players from the hilltop, gave the struggling freshmen fifteen minutes to appear on the gridiron. Eventually the TCU players gave up trying to extricate their ride, and ran to the field—almost an hour and a half late. SMU claimed a 1–0 forfeit victory. TCU vowed, "Just wait till SMU sends a team here. It won't be sent back in the mud and cold; but with a smashing defeat they will long remember."[76] Several Dallas alumni of TCU, including Dan Rogers and Pete Wright, gave the Horned Frogs a banquet for their pains. Probably none of TCU's players from 1918 took the field when the teams next met, three years later.

Denton Normal—a predecessor to the University of North Texas and in those days a teachers' college—made the trip to Fort Worth the next week, and was soundly beaten. "The Teachers" managed only two notable plays—a forty-nine-yard kickoff return at the opening whistle, and a twenty-five-yard pass completion in the fourth quarter. Otherwise it was all TCU from kickoff to the final whistle. Ikey Sanders and Ben Parks each scored twice; Scottie Rutherford and Henderson once. The *Skiff* called the 39–0 win a warm-up for Baylor. Austin College fared little better the following week, having no answer for TCU's talented backfield of Bryan Miller, Irwin, Henderson, and Dave Singletary. Again the *Skiff* called the game a practice for the Baylor game.

Students could get a special fare for a round-trip ticket to Waco for the Thanksgiving game for $2.87, less than half the normal price. The game began with TCU marching downfield to Baylor's goal, and then turning it over on downs only inches from the end zone. Neither team scored in the first half. Bryan Miller opened the scoring in the third quarter with a sixty-five-yard kick return for six points; TCU missed the point after. Baylor took the lead when it recovered a muffed punt (the *Skiff* said Miller signaled fair catch, but the referee would not recognize it) and ran it in for a touchdown. The Bears got the point after, and the one-point lead held until the game's final minutes. By then the fans were filing out. Parks replaced Ervin (maybe "Irvin") at TCU's quarterback position, and after two long incompletions, Parks launched a thirty-five-yard pass to Scottie Rutherford who ran it in for the winning score, TCU up 12–7.

Baylor hurried to get in an answering drive as time ran out. A whistle blew, and TCU claimed a sensational come-from-behind victory. Baylor's coach objected, holding that both the referee's and the timekeeper's whistle (Coach Cahoon's, in this case) had to sound to end a game. Emotions ran high, and before long both coaches were on the field arguing with the referee, Massingill, about whether or not Baylor had snapped the ball before the final whistle. Debate raged over which whistles signaled the end of the game—the referee's or both his and the timekeeper's. The referee did not make a final call on the issue for two hours, but eventually gave a written statement saying TCU was the victor. Baylor's coach sent a misleading telegraph to Walter Camp, asking which official's whistle ended the contest. Camp confirmed that the referee's whistle was the deciding one, settling the debate in TCU's favor.

TCU students, continuing a tradition of burying a Baylor bear after victories over Baylor, made a great show of burying a casket said to contain the Wacoans' mascot after the game. Mischievous-minded Baylor students exhumed the casket in the dark of night after the students had all left for Christmas. The casket, shut fast with seventy-five nails the night of the game, was empty, however, and must have prompted quick action in

Waco, because the *Lariat* reported the bear was again safe at home, even if a little worse for the wear. The *Skiff* got a good laugh.

TCU's improbable wartime success netted the school a second winning season, this year with four wins and three losses. Will Hill Acker, selected for the all-state team, was elected captain for 1919. TCU expected to have Heine Prinzing back on the team, as well as little Dutch Meyer. Meyer's expected return generated more excitement for baseball than for football. (The baseball team won the TIAA again in '19.) That neither would play football at TCU in 1919 was unexpected but not surprising, given the war. That their absence would nearly bring the entire university—not just the football team—to its knees, however, was truly unanticipated.

1919

The next school year began and ended with foment. TCU's remarkable wartime success came to a halt, interrupted not by fighting overseas, but by turbulence on campus. TCU had a new coach for 1919, T. E. D. Hackney—a sensational kicker at Missouri Valley as a player, and afterwards an assistant coach for his alma mater. He had dozens of capable players to work with, including all-state tackle Will Acker, guard Cecil Bradford (TCU's first fourth-year letterman in three years), Dutch Meyer, Astyanax Douglass, Frank Ogilvie, and Heine Prinzing.

The opening of the school year was indelibly marred when TCU denied admission to Frank Ogilvie, the school's leading quarterback and student body president. The administration acted ostensibly in response to the student's involvement in hazing. Hazing had frustrated school officials (and, presumably, other students!) across the state for years. Allegations of excessive hazing emerged at multiple Texas schools throughout the decade.

On the Monday following TCU's refusal to admit Frank Ogilvie, the school suspended or refused admission to five more students, including Heine Prinzing and Dutch Meyer. The action prompted a furious reaction from the student body, and eighty-four men threatened to walk out and join the six suspended students.

Alumni sided with the suspended students, who unsuccessfully appealed to the board of trustees. Thirty-two of the students packed their trunks; the administration threatened not to approve any credits for transfer if the striking students attempted to enroll elsewhere. The threat gave them pause, and they unpacked, but were still barred from attending class. The disruption spread. Students stayed away from both football practice and classes.

Cobby de Stivers, yell leader, from the 1920 yearbook.

The standoff moved to the courts, where the student plaintiffs prayed to enjoin the administration from refusing to admit them. The parties settled before the hearing, allowing the six students to be honorably dismissed from TCU and transfer away. Classes and normalcy resumed. The relief among the students was palpable: they held a remarkably fervent pep rally in which Cobby de Stivers made a name for herself as yell leader and first fan.

Cecil Bradford won the election to fill the vacancy as new student body president. His football team had suffered, however, from the upheaval. Practices had been cancelled during the admissions crisis, a serious hindrance for a relatively young team. Inexperience, distraction, and poor preparation combined to torpedo the Horned Frogs' streak of winning seasons. Among the scant bright spots were two stars who emerged during an otherwise gloomy year of football: lineman Roland "Cowboy" Ogan and quarterback Chester "Boob" Fowler. Ogan was one of TCU's finest-ever linemen, and Fowler TCU's first great throwing quarterback.

The Denton Normal Eagles stymied the Frogs to open the season. The Eagles played superior defense with aggressive blocking and aggressive punching. They racked up penalty yards, some for "slugging" in spades, and repeatedly ran running plays off of quick shift formations to spring their back Cobb free for big yardage. TCU was playing out of character—fumbling often, rushing primarily, and passingly ineffectively—and found itself down two scores at halftime. In the second half, Biss Newman and Rubenstein powered TCU to some success on the ground, and Vaughn Wilson threw a touchdown to Scottie Rutherford. But the rally fizzled, and TCU lost 14–6.

Roland "Cowboy" Ogan.
Photo from the TCU Athletics Association archives.

The next week, rain forced Trinity to postpone its match with TCU, giving Coach Hackney two weeks to prepare for Oklahoma A&M, which he expected to be a bruising match. It was. After a punting duel in the first quarter with the Aggies from Stillwater, TCU found itself forced to defend its goal from only four yards out. The Horned Frogs stiffened, and forced a turnover on downs. TCU lacked a good punter, and being unable to punt themselves out of danger, had to repeat the feat, and again held the orange and black out of the goal, this time from five yards out. This sequence repeated twice more in the second quarter before the Aggies quit trying and attempted a field goal, and missed.

TCU scored first in the third quarter, on a drive that began with Haden blocking an Oklahoma A&M punt. Wilson passed twice to Rutherford, for twenty and then ten yards, which eventually led to a score. A&M held the ball for forty-five minutes in the game, and scored twice in the fourth quarter as TCU's players grew tired of playing defense. TCU lost the slugfest 14-7. The battle riveted the spectators and won TCU praise for "one of the hardest fought and gamest battles that Fort Worth fans have been privileged to see in many a day."[77]

Southwestern was the letdown game, as the Frogs could not muster the same effort that they had brought to Oklahoma A&M. The game was a fumble-ridden punting duel, most memorable for the emergence of Cowboy Ogan as a remarkable tackler at end, playing for the injured Pud Hooser. Down 3–0 shortly before halftime, the Frogs drove the length of the field, and Wilson made what appeared to be a touchdown pass to Rutherford. But the end had stepped out the back of the end zone, and the Pirates got the ball at the twenty, still in the lead. This setback sapped the energy from the Frogs, who did not mount a serious effort on offense until the fourth quarter. TCU's repeated passing attempts failed, and the game closed in a third consecutive loss, 10–0.

Mother nature favored TCU in its rescheduled game with Trinity in Waxahachie. TCU's players had made a pact not to shave until they won a game. Some of their female fans likewise had pledged to wear their hair above their ears until the men shaved. The trip to Waxahachie yielded TCU's first win of the year, although both teams played ineptly for most of the game. Punting, fumbling, and intercepting the other team's passes were the orders of the day through three quarters. TCU missed a field goal attempt in the first half; Trinity only threatened to score early in the first quarter.

Center Joel Haden at last broke the logjam when he broke through Trinity's line to block and recover a punt. He rumbled fifteen yards for the game's sole touchdown. Will Acker made the point after, and the game was as good as over. TCU nearly doubled the score when a Trinity trick play went awry in the fourth quarter. Typically, the Tigers passed out of a handoff—like a play action pass following a handoff—only this time the Trinity handoff accidently went to TCU lineman Oscar Mayo, who promptly began running downfield, unobstructed. The referee inexplicably blew the play dead and was himself unable to explain why. TCU failed to score on that drive, or on a drive that was boosted by a sixty-yard scamper by Chester "Boob" Fowler. The game finished 7–0.

Despite the victory, morale among students and team was low. The usual fiery pep rallies at chapel before games had withered, and game attendance with it. Instead of vigorous, organized cheering, the team played to a lethargic and increasingly hostile home crowd. Even the half-time snake dance suffered. Those fans that did attend the games were disgruntled. Their catcalls stung. The *Skiff* ran a large ad following the Trinity game, calling those student fans yellow who themselves called the players yellow.

TCU's offense, which had sputtered all season, went entirely absent in Sherman against Austin College. The team missed Scottie Rutherford and Biss Newman, who did not start. The Kangaroos scored the game's only points before halftime on a forty-five-yard touchdown pass. Both teams leaned increasingly on the pass to move the ball late in the game; neither

Captain Will Hill Acker
was named "Most Popular" in the TCU yearbook.

succeeded. Will Acker and Joel Haden both were injured. TCU lost 6–0.

Texas A&M called next, in Fort Worth. The Aggies had not been scored on all season, and kept that streak intact with their romp with the Horned Frogs. A&M made twenty-one first downs, and held TCU to only two. Guard Oscar Mayo made multiple tackles behind A&M's line, but the Farmers played relentlessly, winning 48–0.

Captain Acker implored the fans to show up and shout for the home team in the season finale against Baylor: "Wake up, TCU. Where is your pep? . . . Everything that we are in the way of athletics depends on whether we win this game or not."[78] Some coeds led a resurgence of school spirit—first Gertrude Davies before the trip to Austin College, and in the last week of the season Cobby de Stivers, the female yell leader. Her antics in anticipation drew mention in the *Dallas Morning News*, and it turned the tide on campus, finally drawing out the enthusiasm for the football team that TCU had become accustomed to. Despite the bitter cold, TCU students paraded through Fort Worth prior to the Thanksgiving game with a caged bear in tow. Their pregame fervor stunned Baylor's fans.

TCU played near full strength. Pud Hooser was back from injury, but did not return to his former starting end position; he played in the backfield instead. During the game itself, fans felt aggrieved by the officials, who penalized the Frogs at every opportunity. Umpire John Touchstone, SMU's assistant coach whom the *Skiff* lauded as reputably fair only weeks earlier, drew the most ire. By the time TCU had been docked almost two

Chester "Boob" Fowler, TCU's first
great passing quarterback.

hundred yards in penalties in the first half, the *Skiff* was ready to name
him "the worst official ever seen on Clark Field."[79] Nevertheless, the Frog
defense played magnificently, and Boob Fowler's punting, which had been
a liability early in the season, had become a strength. TCU held Baylor
scoreless despite defending the Bears in the red zone in heavy mud most of
the first quarter. In the second quarter, Baylor managed to score on a drive
of four long end runs in succession, the last a twenty-five-yard scamper
around Cowboy Ogan, breaking five tackles en route to the end zone. TCU
drove to Baylor's twenty with passes to Jazz Cunningham before halftime,
which featured rival snake dances from the fans. Five hundred TCU fans
took the field for their dance, complete with canes and horns, chanting,
"T-rah, T-rah, T-C-U-rah!"

TCU held the Bears in Baylor territory through most of the second
half. Boob Fowler had several large gains negated by penalties assessed
by Touchstone—one for hurdling that even drew a complaint from another
official. Both defenses were strong in their respective red zones. TCU drove
to Baylor's twenty-yard line but lost possession on an attempted touchdown
pass. Baylor drove to TCU's sixteen, at which point a "kneeing" penalty
from Touchstone brought the crowd onto the field, irate and pleading with
Coach Hackney to withdraw from the game in protest. His players helped
the police corral the crowd, and the game continued to its 7–0 finish. The
same police escorted Touchstone through the riot that erupted at the final
whistle. The *Skiff* claimed even Baylor's players said the calls against

TCU were unfair. So hot was the contempt for Touchstone that TCU's fans and writers found good things to say about Baylor, especially its star back "Smiling Nig" Dotson, who had run rings about TCU's ends all day. A year would pass before the *Lariat* could bring itself to mention the controversy.

4
CHAMPIONS

1920

The 1920 season dawned bright. The war had been over for nearly a year. Notwithstanding the disappointing exit of Fred Cahoon from the team and the school, optimism about the Horned Frogs' prospects percolated through the student body. The new coach, Billy Driver, and assistant John McKnight impressed onlookers with strenuous workouts. The team had not held preseason workouts without Coach Cahoon since 1912.

Several players who had been absent from the school a year or more returned and played well in preseason drills—tackle (and kicker) Troy Haire, Dutch Meyer (reenrolled and considered one of the loudest men in school), center Astyanax Douglass, and Bryan Miller. Haire led an experienced team. Meyer and Douglass joined Acker as all-state alums on the line; Meyer took over Cowboy Ogan's spot at left end, and Ogan replaced Paul Lockman at fullback.

Returning players from the 1919 squad, Roland "Cowboy" Ogan, tackle Red Spiller, guard Oscar Mayo, Chester Fowler, and Colvern Henry drew praise early. Notable freshmen included quarterback Earl Stegall from North Side High, tackle Loren Houtchens of Riverside (or Fort Worth Central), Gilbert P. Jackson from Dalhart, Pete Fulcher—who had played with a military team that won acclaim—and fullback Raleigh "Rab" Ryan from Bonham. The *Skiff* declared the team superior to Baylor on the strength of preseason workouts alone.

Heine Prinzing, also reenrolled, cheered the spirits of the 1920 team merely by showing up to practice. In a baseball game in the spring, he had collided with Astyanax Douglass and fallen unconscious. Prinzing hovered near death for several weeks. Against all medical odds, he returned to school in 1920 and expected to be able to play football again. He was the elected captain for 1920, but had to quit before fall camp was over. Troy Haire from Granger was elected captain in his place.

On the wider horizon, clouds were gathering over the TIAA. Most Southwest Conference teams declined to schedule TCU, which played in an inferior conference. The TIAA allowed its schools to play freshmen; the Southwest Conference did not. More importantly, however, the Southwest Conference already was a prestige conference, and the TIAA was not. Texas A&M and Baylor each would play the Fort Worth school once more, but only SMU would maintain its series with the Frogs. Even this cross-town series was rumored to be ending when SMU joined the Southwest Conference in 1922. Baylor stopped scheduling TCU for its Thanksgiving game, opting instead for a Southwest Conference foe: SMU. The schools' attempt to start a Baylor-SMU Thanksgiving rivalry left TCU in the awkward quest for a new turkey day tradition. TCU was being forced out of its traditional football family.

FOOTBALL

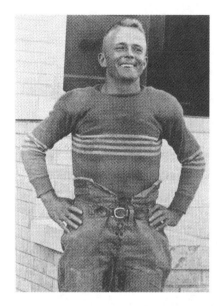
The inimitable Dutch Meyer, 1919.

Fort Worth's business community, which still included all of West Texas, did not shy away from the Frogs. Porter Whaley of the West Texas Chamber of Commerce prominently supported TCU football in 1920. Stewart Bassett, a local businessman, promised the team a silver cup if it beat Baylor.

TCU made innovative plans to end the season with an exhibition game with an out-of-town team. This oddity—a "postseason" game—was tentatively scheduled with the famous Praying Colonels of Centre College, from Danville, Kentucky. Centre College had captured America's attention by beating then-dominant Harvard. The Colonels won their nickname by praying on the field. Before each game, the team captain would select a player to pray in a huddle on the field—never for Centre College to win, but for protection against injuries and for the best team to win. In 1919 Centre outscored its opponents by over 400 to 18. In its era, the team resembled the giant-slaying Boise State Broncos—with Ian Johnson and Kellen Moore—in the first decade of the twenty-first century. (Later in the 1920 season Harvard and Georgia Tech beat the Praying Colonels, however, taking some of the luster off the Kentucky sensation.)

The Centre College football team was closely connected to Texas and to Fort Worth. The coach, Charlie Moran, had coached and umpired baseball in Texas for years, and coached football at Texas A&M. His son Tommie punted for the Praying Colonels.

Team photo, 1921.

Charlie Moran stocked his Centre College team with players from Texas and the southwest. The leader of the group was returning Walter Camp all-American quarterback Bo McMillin. McMillin graduated from Fort Worth's North Side High School, and may still be Fort Worth's most illustrious football son. He was a solid tackler who could stop on a dime and throw the ball long. He led a passing offense that no team up to this point had stopped.

Few opponents could contrast less favorably with such a marquee opponent than the Horned Frogs' season opening foe, Southeastern Normal College (now Southeastern Oklahoma State University), from Durant, Oklahoma. Austin College had beaten the hapless Oklahomans 62–0 the week prior. Austin College had retained much of its championship team from 1919, and loomed as likely the toughest match on the Frogs' 1920 schedule. The Horned Frogs considered their performance versus SNC to be a barometer of their chances the next week against the Kangaroos.

The Frogs line-plunged consistently against the Oklahomans for two scores in the first quarter, and then repeatedly came up short of touchdowns by inches in the second and third quarters. The teams tallied many unnecessary roughness penalties; one pushed the Frogs back fifty yards. Then Astyanax Douglass blocked a kick which Dutch Meyer scooped up and ran in for the game's final score. The Frogs won 20–0.

The Kangaroos ran a short pass offense that was unusual in its day and were 1-1 coming into the match with TCU, having been bested by Baylor on a fluky play the prior week. Coach Driver juggled his lineup for the game: Oscar Mayo for Stevenson, Cowboy Ogan for Henry, Gilbert P. Jackson for Boob Fowler, Fowler for Judge Green, and Rab Ryan in Ogan's place at fullback. At first, the changes appeared to weaken the squad. The Kangaroos opened the game by driving through the Horned Frogs like a hot knife through butter, quickly putting the first score on the board. But thereafter the Horned Frogs shone, especially on defense. TCU blocked multiple passes and drove the ball with old–fashioned blocking and running, scoring in the second quarter. Will Acker missed the point after, so TCU was still behind by a point for a few minutes before Acker made a field goal to make the score 9–7 at halftime.

TCU's defense stifled several Austin College punt returns in the second half. Austin College held TCU at the goal line multiple times. The outcome hinged on two would-be field goals that the Kangaroos' kicker missed, either one of which would have been the winning points. TCU won, and the bitter Kangaroos accused TCU of buying the referee. The *Skiff* took exception.

Because the Horned Frogs were convinced that Austin College was the best team in the state, beating the Kangaroos fired them with confidence for the remainder of the schedule. With thoughts of beating Baylor five games down the line already in its mind, TCU travelled to Arkansas for its first game in the Gem State. Arkansas was known for solid defense, and it played up to its reputation to open the game. The Razorbacks blocked a TCU punt at the goal line and soon after registered a safety. The Razorback's Harris was successful on end runs, one for thirty yards coming just a yard shy of six points. TCU then scored all but two of the game's remaining points before halftime, at which point Coach Driver let up, and defense ruled in the second half. TCU won 19–2.

TCU went next to Waxahachie to play Trinity on a Tuesday and was again heavily favored. The weekday game (which about 150 students missed some classes to attend) began with a punting duel. TCU's left halfback Allen Rowson averaged forty-five yards per punt on the day. TCU blew the game open in the second quarter, Rab Ryan plunging for the first touchdown on a short yardage play. Trinity then stopped TCU twice near its goal, punting the ball into midfield, but could not stop TCU's third drive. Will Acker ran after a catch to the goal line, and again Ryan plunged for the score. Acker scored a third touchdown before halftime on a thirty-five-yard fumble recovery; he also kicked the point after. Trinity scored its only points shortly after halftime. The game then returned to its defensive character, dampened by a cold front that blew a windy drizzle

Allen Rowson.
Photo from the TCU Athletics Association archives.

into the game and numbed players and fans alike. By the final whistle, the players could not see the whitewashed ball in the darkness.

The bye week, although well timed, did not give sufficient time for all of the Frogs' injuries to heal. When Phillips University (also run by the Disciples of Christ) came to Fort Worth, linemen Pete Fulcher and Troy Haire were not expected to play. Fulcher beat expectations and started, but Haire did not. He missed a defensive slugfest led by end Dutch Meyer, who harassed the Oklahomans relentlessly. Phillips, known for its punter Manderville and its pass-heavy attack, completed none of its nine attempts through the air; in like fashion, TCU missed on all three of its pass attempts. TCU made only six first downs; Phillips managed nine. Both teams fumbled abundantly—Phillips once at its own fifteen, giving the Frogs a short field that they promptly fumbled away. Neither team gained consecutive first downs to extend a drive. TCU did drive to Phillips's twelve- and three-yard lines before turning the ball over on downs, but Phillips never got within TCU's thirty-five-yard line. Allen Rowson matched his famous counterpart punting, and Will Acker kicked a thirty-five-yard goal in the second quarter for the game's only points. TCU's pep squad made the gaudiest play of the game when it led a cow across the field with a sign reading, "We're going to beat Phillips; this ain't no bull."

The fans, the newspaper, and presumably the team were focused on Baylor when the Missouri Osteopaths team came to town during a national convention of osteopaths. The doctors from Kirksville outweighed the Frogs on average, and nearly upset the streaking purple. Three would-be starters, Rowson, Spiller, and Houtchens, did not play. Gilbert Jackson fumbled twice in the opening minutes of the game, giving the Bonesetters a short field. Escaping the jam having given up only a field goal, the Frog defense held the Bonesetters in their own territory for the remainder of the game. Wylie Harris started the Frogs' first scoring drive with twelve minutes remaining in the game, rushing for fifteen yards, then receiving a pass from Boob Fowler for twelve more. Fowler and Rab Ryan finished the job on the ground, to give the Frogs their first lead of the day.

Gilbert Jackson redeemed himself with a sensational fifty-yard kick return later in the quarter to give the Frogs a short field; TCU made the most of the opportunity, scoring on a Rab Ryan rush with six minutes to play. Jackson nearly hauled in another touchdown as time expired, this time on a pass from Fowler, but the referee said the halfback had stepped out of bounds at the goal and would not count the score. TCU's 13–3 victory was the team's sixth straight.

By now the winning streak had entirely erased the complacency that plagued the TCU campus in 1919. The team and school had focused on the Baylor game all season. TCU sewed imitation footballs on the uniform (under the arm) of each player. On the weekend of the game three hundred students (a third of TCU's typical enrollment) and roughly one hundred fans from Fort Worth took a special train to Waco to watch the rivalry.

Waco's home crowd—over seven thousand in the Cotton Palace—dwarfed the TCU contingent. TCU probably never had played before a crowd so large. When the teams took the field on the wintry and windy afternoon, Baylor (or the officials) requested the Horned Frogs remove the imitation footballs. TCU obliged, and at last the game could begin.

Baylor opened the game with an onside kick, but TCU drew first blood late in the first quarter (perhaps early in the second) after Rab Ryan and Wylie Harris drove to Baylor's thirty. Boob Fowler passed to Dutch Meyer for the score. In the second quarter, Astyanax Douglass intercepted a Baylor pass at the Bears' thirty-five-yard line. Jackson ran for fifteen, but the drive stalled after neither Ryan nor Harris could gain much on the ground up the middle. Baylor thought it had escaped the threat when it blocked Acker's kick, but TCU recovered the ball for a first down. Fowler lobbed a touchdown to Jackson on the next play, and the Frogs went into halftime up two scores. The *Lariat* called TCU's first-half touchdowns "lucky" lobs into the end zone.[80] Lucky or not, the home crowd never had

Raleigh "Rab" Ryan.
Photo from the TCU Athletics Association archives.

much to cheer for; the travelling fans made them sound "like a soloist in a boiler factory."[81] The teams traded touchdowns in the fourth (Baylor's came on a sixty-yard scamper by Nig Dotson), and TCU went home winners, 21–9. Allen Rowson impressed the *Lariat* as the best Horned Frog on the field, able to get yards on the ground almost at will. The *Skiff* pronounced its team unbeatable. And for two more weeks, it was.

The Simmons College Cowboys from Abilene could not corral Allen Rowson, who ran for sixty-five-yard touchdowns twice, and powered TCU to a 31–2 win. Rowson did not play further in 1920 because the TIAA president ruled him ineligible for further competition. The halfback had registered—but apparently did not play—at A&M in 1919.

TCU's first Thanksgiving game in five years against a team other than Baylor featured the Southwestern Pirates, who very nearly put a black mark on TCU's regular season. Both teams had mostly recovered from the season's accumulation of injuries. The game opened with something like a homecoming court, featuring Miss Christina Thurmond, whom the *Skiff* called the "sponsor" of TCU football for the season, and a retinue of five coeds. Miss Thurmond made the opening kickoff.

The Pirates stifled TCU's offense through three quarters. The Frogs'

Rab Ryan plunging for ten yards.

only score at that point had come on a tremendous punt return by Rab Ryan in the first quarter. With TCU trailing 16–7 midway through the fourth quarter, some fans thought the game already over in the gathering darkness, and filed out. Then Boob Fowler got loose for forty yards (maybe fifty)—only to be tackled two yards shy of the goal line. Rab Ryan plunged into the end zone on the next play, and the rally was on. Acker kicked the point after, narrowing Southwestern's lead to two points. Managing a pass attack in the darkness was a challenge, but Gilbert Jackson (subbing for left halfback Wylie Harris) hauled in Fowler's first pass, and ran it all the way for the winning score. TCU won 21–16, and for the second time won a conference championship.

While racking up wins in its longest streak to date, the assistant athletic director, Professor Fox, travelled to Danville, Kentucky, and finalized plans with Centre College to play TCU in Fort Worth after the season. Fox also secured Centre College's promise to play TCU following the 1921 season, as well.

Postseason games—or bowl games, to use an anachronism—had yet to take root in college sports. The Rose Bowl began to feature college football games annually only a few years before. Fans would wait another decade for the Sugar or Orange Bowls. TCU students converted their enthusiasm for their team's undefeated season into plans to attend the extra game. So many of them planned to return to campus early to attend the game that the school moved final exams and the start date for the spring semester up two days. The announcement of these changes drew laughter from the student body.

Expectations, of course, could not be tethered. The papers called the game a "classic" even though a postseason exhibition was unprecedented outside California. Fans and alumni of both schools swamped TCU's administration with requests for tickets. The Horned Frogs built temporary stands for ten thousand spectators at Panther Park. The bowl game was an idea whose time was ripe.

Acclaim for the Praying Colonels' Bo McMillin led a *Star-Telegram* writer to suggest that Centre was a one-man team, likely to fall when it met a more balanced team like TCU's.[82] The paper did not note Centre College's "Four Aces" backfield, which featured three other talented backs with McMillin: Armstrong, Tanner, and Bartlett.

The game probably drew the first national attention to TCU football. Fans and tourists came on trains from all over the country to see the game, and jammed North Main Street with automobile traffic. The *Dallas Morning News* called it the largest crowd ever to attend an athletic event in Fort Worth.[83]

TCU installed silent signals for the match, practicing them for a few days after final exams. Center Astyanax Douglass gave the signals. The game began well for TCU—one of McMillin's first passes bounced off the fingers of a receiver and into Gilbert Jackson's waiting arms; Jackson ran seventy yards down the sideline untouched for the first score. But the Colonels brought a more physically punishing game to Fort Worth than the Frogs expected. Allen Rowson had to be carried off the field in the first quarter; Jackson and Boob Fowler each left on a stretcher, Fowler with a broken ankle.

Following Jackson's long touchdown, the Colonels pounded the Frogs for long gains—fifteen, fourteen, six, and twenty yards—and suddenly TCU was defending its goal line, hoping to prevent a tie. TCU's silent signals must not have been the only change made for the game: instead of passing to drive the ball, Centre College pounded the ball at the reeling Frogs. They bucked in for the tying score, blocked TCU's punt at the five-yard line on its next possession, and then took the lead.

TCU shot itself in the foot on a punt when Astyanax Douglass snapped the ball over the punter; the Frogs recovered the ball but were unable to convert. They turned the ball over on downs to give Centre College a short field, and the opportunistic Colonels quickly scored again. TCU finished the first quarter by throwing an interception, giving Centre a short field and an easy score to open the second quarter. Up 28–7, the Praying Colonels gained yards on an off-tackle run with ease—McMillin ran for seventy-five yards and a touchdown using the play. The bleeding continued unabated in the second half, when Centre added five scores before the final whistle, winning 63-7.

Instead of ending their championship season with a nation-shocking upset, the Horned Frogs had to take solace, if any could be found, in two facts: Bo McMillin said TCU tackled him as hard on his last run as it did on his first, and the Frogs held Centre College's vaunted passing attack to only three completions in twenty tries. The first accolade, given during McMillin's postgame interview, may have been good sportsmanship more than fact. And the statistics on Centre's passing game ignores the Praying Colonels' obliteration of TCU's rush defense. Few seasons in Fort Worth would rise to such heights, only to fall to such depths.

1921

For the first time in eleven seasons, the 1921 Horned Frogs fielded an experienced team at the opener, both in the coaching staff and players. In 1921, Coaches Driver and McKnight both returned to coach a team that started eleven returning lettermen. Not since 1909 had TCU featured a returning coach and more returning players than new ones. In 1915, the returning lettermen outnumbered the first year lettermen, but the coaching staff was new. The stability on the 1921 roster did not obscure instability in the team's position among Texas schools, however. The Horned Frogs considered requesting admission to the Southwest Conference. It was an open secret that the school planned to make a formal application to join the more prestigious group of schools at the conference's annual meeting in December.

Dutch Meyer took over at quarterback, and Cowboy Ogan took over at center. The team practiced a full week in Canyon, Texas—near Amarillo—prior to the opener with West Texas State Normal College, so that the TCU players would be accustomed to the difference in altitude, and, said the coach, so they could take advantage of the swimming holes in Palo Duro Canyon.[84]

The season opened with a bang—a tremendous hailstorm rolled over Amarillo and West Texas State's football park at the opening whistle, scattering the players and fans. When the storm blew over, Dutch Meyer returned the kickoff, and the Frogs drove the field with line plunges by Rab Ryan and Boob Fowler and end runs by Fowler. The Frogs scored on this opening drive four minutes later. Meyer, playing quarterback, mixed in passes on the next drive, including one to Gilbert Jackson for a touchdown. TCU scored a third time before the first quarter was over. Up 20–0 at the half, Coach Driver put in his second team, and a new halfback named Homer Adams impressed with his physical running and a score. Cowboy Ogan drew plaudits for his work in the trenches, and Heine Prinzing played well with the second team in his first football game in two years. TCU won the opener 30–0.

On the road again in Abilene, the Horned Frogs played Simmons College on a field that had been freshly plowed and harrowed. The long trip to Abilene tired the team, and the rough ground slowed TCU's backfield.

TCU—0, Phillips—0 (1921).

Led by their quarterback Yeager, the Cowboys beat the Horned Frogs 10–7. TCU students rallied around the team for the next week's game, but were disappointed again when TCU lost a shootout to Oklahoma A&M in Stillwater. TCU scored first, on steady ground gains by Ryan and Fowler in the first quarter. Oklahoma A&M scored the next three touchdowns, however, and TCU never recovered the lead, losing 28–21.

Trinity came to Panther Park the following week and lost 19-3 in a game that was not as close as the score indicated. Boob Fowler made the play of the game when he ran forty yards for a touchdown early in the first quarter; halftime stopped TCU only a yard away from the Tigers' goal. TCU fumbled away a possession in the red zone in the second half, then scored a second time on a line buck by Rab Ryan. Like the first half, the second closed with TCU holding the ball within Trinity's one-yard line.

In Fort Worth the following week, TCU handed Tulsa its first loss in several years. Tulsa threatened to score twice in the first quarter, but TCU held the Hurricanes off both times and picked up a safety in the second quarter by downing Tulsa's punt returner (and quarterback) Keck in his own end zone. Boob Fowler passed to Blair Cherry for a touchdown on the Frogs' next possession, to go up 9–0. Rab Ryan plunged for a second score after halftime, and TCU won the game 16–0.

After playing Phillips University in Enid, Oklahoma, to a rainy, fight-ridden, scoreless tie the following week, TCU squared off with the Missouri Osteopaths. The Frogs' defense had not allowed a team into the red zone for several weeks running, but could not hold that remarkable streak against the doctors from Kirksville. The weather was unseasonably warm, souring the outlook for the Osteopaths, who were favored to win but were accustomed to playing in cold weather. The Bonesetter's quarterback Sermon was something of a sensation, and played well against the Horned Frogs. But TCU's defense, led by big left guard McConnell who stopped

Lettermen's Association, 1920–1921.

the Bonesetters behind the line several times, kept the Missouri team out of the end zone. The match was low scoring and hard hitting; Rab Ryan and Homer Adams each left the game with injuries. When Cowboy Ogan picked up a muffed pass in the last quarter, thinking it was a fumble, and ran seventy yards before being tackled, he thought he was going to double the score. The roaring crowd was quieted when the referee called the ball an incomplete pass, nixing the play. Eventually the doctors wilted in the warm weather, and could not contain TCU's backfield of Fowler, Adams, Honey, and Camp. The Horned Frogs powered to the end zone, and won 7–0.

SMU fielded its best team to date in 1921, with a line that was as heavy as TCU's. The Mustangs' Coach Rix resigned in October, and SMU hired William Cunningham to lead the team for the remainder of the season. (Ray Morrison—the school's first athletic director and football coach—had been an assistant coach, and would lead the program again in 1922.) Cunningham brought his team to Fort Worth to see TCU play the Bonesetters. He hired Choc Kelly, a Fort Worth regular, to help his team. Kelly was considered one of TCU's most knowledgeable fans, and the hire prompted Coach Driver to hold TCU's practices prior to the SMU game in secret. Nevertheless, Cunningham's strategy nearly worked. SMU held TCU to two scores in the first half, including a Boob Fowler thirty-five-yard touchdown toss to Loren Houtchens in the second quarter.

TCU—13, SMU—6 (1921).

Before halftime, the Frogs recovered an SMU fumble at their own twenty-five-yard line and drove more than sixty yards—mostly in small ground gains—but could not convert in the red zone. SMU narrowed the score to 13–6 with a long touchdown pass early in the third, and pressed the Frogs for the remainder of the quarter (garnering eighty yards in one run near the end). But both defenses held, and neither team scored again.

TCU's winning streak came to an end when Matty Bell's Haskell College Indians came to Fort Worth. They brought a wet cold front with them, which drove fans away and dampened the Frogs' passing attack. Despite the weather, the Horned Frogs drove to the Indians' goal four times in the first half, but never could push the ball over. In the second half, which began scoreless, TCU's luck ran out, and the Frogs lost by two scores. Cowboy Ogan, playing center, made tackle after tackle behind the line.

Arkansas came to town to play TCU on Thanksgiving—a second year for the Horned Frogs to play the traditional game against a nontraditional foe. Fans packed the stands for the Thanksgiving game against the out-of-state team. The Razorbacks found themselves in a jam near the end of the first quarter, and were only able to punt the ball to about their thirty-yard line. Given the short field, Boob Fowler passed to Houtchens inside the ten, and the quarter ended with TCU threatening to score. Rab Ryan ran in for the game's opening score to open the second quarter; TCU missed the point after. Arkansas answered on its next drive, and by making the point after the touchdown, took the lead.

Blair Cherry sat out most of the first half injured, but Coach Driver sent him in for the second half, when Cherry and Camp both received long passes from Boob Fowler to set up the Frogs' second touchdown—a one-yard plunge from Fowler to take the lead. Spurred by the Frogs' score, Arkansas again drove the field and scored in response. In the fourth

TCU–19, Arkansas–14 (1921).

quarter, Fowler engineered another scoring drive primarily with passes to Cherry and to Hillard Camp, then finished the job himself with a rushing touchdown to give TCU the 19–14 win. The *Skiff* was profuse in its praise of the Razorbacks' sportsmanship; the only penalty of the game was a holding call against Arkansas.

In a way, beating Arkansas for a sixth win in 1921 marked the end of TCU's climax years of early football. The postseason rematch with Centre College did not occur. Boob Fowler forsook a fourth year in college to join former Frogs Astyanax Douglass and Pete Donahue on the Cincinnati Reds. Coach Driver would not return, either to coach or to lead the athletic department. Judge Green was chosen captain for the 1922 squad. His team would not win many games, but would usher the program out of the TIAA and into a new conference filled with old foes. The move mirrored TCU's wandering among conferences eighty years later.

1922

Football was maturing into the game that current audiences would recognize, so it's easy to forget that American college life still had not made that same lurch into modernity. A humorous notice in a 1922 edition of the *Skiff* highlights that social contrast. The report announces a curious club among TCU men that year, one that called itself the "Public Primpers," with the motto "Privacy Be Darned." These lads were offended when girls put on makeup in public, and vowed to shame the coeds by returning the favor. Whenever one of them spotted a lass applying powder or lipstick, he would open his bag, produce a large comb, and run it through his mustache. "If he has no mustache he shall bring out a pair of military

Homer Adams, 1921.

hair brushes and slick his hair. If he has no hair he shall take out a whisk broom and brush his clothes. If he has no clothes he shall bring forth a blackening brush and polish his shoes. If he has no shoes he shall produce a small tub with water, soap, and washrag and take a bath."[85]

Football at TCU in 1922 got off to an earlier-than-usual start with TCU's first foray into a very modern practice: spring football. Previously, spring football had been an intramural event that usually did not feature varsity players, but in 1922 spring drills matured into an extension of summer football camp. The practices convinced Cowboy Ogan and Gilbert Jackson, who had been on the fence about whether or not to return to the gridiron, to play again for the Frogs. Jackson and Homer Adams were expected to be the speedy halfbacks, and Cranfill the heavy line plunger.

In the fall, Jackson changed his mind again and did not play. The *Skiff* looked to Doc Livsey to take Loren Houtchens place opposite Blair Cherry at end. In preseason drills, Cherry expected to play in the backfield. Bill Honey worked at quarterback before the season began, but new head coach John McKnight chose left-handed Homer Adams for throwing the ball once the season started. McKnight had been the assistant coach for a couple of years, and knew his players well.

Pete Wright resigned his position with Southwest National Bank of Dallas to take over the athletic director position at TCU, vacated by W. L. Driver. Wright revived the push to leave the TIAA for the Southwest Conference. The move would be a homecoming of sorts, as the University of Texas, Texas A&M, Baylor, Rice, and SMU were already playing in the new conference.

After a couple of exhibitions against high schools, TCU opened the football season in Dallas against the Dallas University Hilltoppers and played only one freshman, end Lawrence Tankersley. The Catholics also hoped to switch conferences—they had applied to join the TIAA. Their air attack had a good reputation, but was fruitless against the Frogs. Down 14–0 in the fourth, Dallas finally scored on its seventh try from one yard out. Blair Cherry recaptured momentum for TCU, however, by returning Dallas's punt ninety-five yards for the game's final score. TCU won by two touchdowns, disappointing the locals who had congregated for their school's fifteenth anniversary.

TCU prepared to travel the Fort Worth and Denver Railroad to Wichita Falls to face the Simmons Cowboys. Wichita Falls rallied around the team from Abilene; placards for the game hung in almost every store. The contest was a battle of equals, fought on a dusty and hot afternoon. The referees shortened each quarter to twelve minutes on account of the weather. The teams traded punts three times to open the game, until TCU was penalized five yards. The penalty angered Homer Adams, who ran the next play forty-five yards through a maze of defenders for a score. In the third quarter, TCU fumbled near its goal to give Simmons a first and goal, and shortly thereafter allowed the tying score. Neither team scored again. Bill Honey threw an interception in the game's closing minutes, and in the scrum that followed Cowboy Ogan was knocked unconscious. The Frogs first thought he had been seriously hurt and carried him off the field. He recovered quickly, however, and the game ended in a 7–7 tie.

Daniel Baker came to Fort Worth the next week to face a depleted TCU. The Horned Frogs did not play either first team end—Ralph Cantrell and Lawrence Tankersley—and were worse for it. Animosity seems always to have accompanied these schools' games; the fans fought at halftime when some Hillbillies grabbed balloons that TCU's pep squad had used for its halftime routine. With order restored, TCU held a 13–7 lead until the Hillbillies ran off two quick scores in the last minutes of the game for a come-from-behind win. That no players were injured seemed to the *Skiff* to indicate TCU was playing in fine form. But after a tiring train ride to Tulsa the following week, the uninjured Frogs took the field in a red sandstorm and were shut out, 21–0. McKnight called his team's effort the best of the year.[86]

The losing streak prompted a change in hairdos on campus. As they did in 1918, the football players and many of the male students stopped shaving until the team won, while the girls showed solidarity with the team in their hairdos, combed to show their ears.[87] They did not have to

Blair Cherry, 1921.

wait long to revert to normal hygiene. After a parade downtown, TCU defeated Oklahoma A&M in Fort Worth the next week. Adams and Cherry each scored in the second half, and the Frogs nearly scored a third touchdown after blocking an A&M kick. TCU won 22-14.

The next match in Sherman figured to be a game of heavyweights. Austin College had beaten Daniel Baker, SMU, Howard Payne, and Simmons with a strong running game and very efficient line work. The Kangaroos attended TCU's bout against Oklahoma A&M to scout the Frogs, and their study was fruitful. In Sherman the next week, Austin College beat TCU 20–7. More than three thousand fans made the trip from Fort Worth and were in no mood to let the twenty-point halftime deficit ruin their fun. They celebrated on the field in the intermission with remarkable gaiety, staging a fake football game of their own and parading around a Maypole. The Horned Frogs played much better in the second half, using passes from Adams to Camp and Cherry to drive the field. Cherry made a sensational touchdown catch against a barbed wire fence for the Frogs' only score.

The Howard Payne Yellow Jackets travelled from Brownwood to Fort Worth next, and quickly got up fourteen points in the first quarter before the Horned Frogs made any noise. Fullback Kit Carson subbed in for Bill Honey in the second quarter and galloped for a twenty-yard gain from midfield. Meads finished the drive with a touchdown run on the next snap, and kicked the point after. After halftime, TCU twice held Howard Payne at the Horned Frog goal line, the second time recovering a Yellow Jacket

Left to right, from the top: Kit Carson, Dick Fender, Pete Fulcher, Lawrence Tankersley. Photos from the TCU Athletics Association archives.

fumble and punting the ball to the twenty-five. The boys from Brownwood would not be stopped, however, and after two incomplete passes, threw a touchdown to put TCU down again by two scores. Homer Adams made a remarkable interception to jumpstart TCU's second scoring drive, but it was too little, too late: TCU lost 26–14.

Trinity hoped to notch its first victory over the Frogs since 1903 in Waxahachie the following week. TCU moved the ball consistently (gaining eighteen more first downs than Trinity), but neither team crossed the plane more than once. Trinity nearly got its coveted second win, but had to settle for a 7–7 tie. W. E. McConnell and Lindsey Jacks left the game with injuries.

TCU took Thanksgiving to Manhattan, Kansas, to play the Kansas Aggies for the first time. For thirty minutes, the game was a battle with the wind as much as with each other. Kansas did not attempt its signature passing game in the first half, and both teams relied instead on punting to keep out of danger. The half ended in a scoreless tie. TCU's fortunes soured when the teams switched sides at halftime, giving Kansas the wind at its back. The Aggies drove with runs to open the second half, and scored three times in the third quarter. One of Tricky Ward's punts sailed the gale winds for ninety-two yards. Up 26–0, the Aggies sent in their subs, who found TCU so tired that they could score almost as easily as the first team. The match ended with Kansas up 45–0.

Somehow the blowout loss near the end of a mediocre season did not dampen TCU's case before the Southwest Conference.[88] The conference accepted the Horned Frogs' application at its annual meeting, effective immediately. TCU was allowed to play the freshmen currently enrolled, along with those who would enroll for the spring semester. The conference also adjusted its baseball and basketball schedules to include TCU. TCU's football journey, begun in Waco against the legacy teams of Texas, had come full circle. What better way to mark the Horned Frogs' return to its traditional rivalries than a season-ending match with SMU? The game couldn't be held on Thanksgiving, which had passed the week before, but it appropriately inaugurated TCU's entrance into its new conference.

Both SMU's and TCU's athletic directors had to labor to rebut newspaper reports in Fort Worth and Dallas that the season finale between the two teams was cancelled in 1922.[89] Coach McKnight looked forward to fielding a healthy team. Like the game a week and a half before in Kansas, the first half was a punting duel and a scoreless tie. Unlike the disaster in Manhattan, the SMU game continued to the end as a scoreless tie. SMU only completed one pass all game. The Mustangs nearly won on what appeared to be a seventy-yard touchdown run late in the fourth quarter, but the ballcarrier stepped out of bounds and the referee called his score back.

From the 1922 *Horned Frog* yearbook.

Bright days awaited TCU in the Southwest Conference. The Game of the Century and a Heisman Trophy dazzled in the distance. Frantic Francis Schmidt would give style to TCU football. One of Fort Worth's favorite sons, Dutch Meyer, would return to make a new name for himself as a coach—the Saturday Fox—and twice take his alma mater to the top of the polls. TCU would become, in truth, the prince of the Southwest in the 1930s, and then, with the unassuming Abe Martin, would share the title with the Longhorns in the 1950s.

Then, slowly, the program would descend into mediocrity and irrelevance. The Big Eight and the politically connected Texas programs left the little Fort Worth school for dead when they broke up the Southwest Conference and formed the Big 12. The revival under Gary Patterson shines all the more brilliantly for its contrast with the decades that preceded it, and for the homecoming it created for TCU in the Big 12. TCU always finds its way home to the new place its friends have made.

But these are all stories for another day.

Inaugural Season, 1896 (1-1-1)
Toby's Business College W 8-6
at Houston Heavyweights L 0-22
Houston Heavyweights T 0-0

1897 (3-1)
at East Dallas W 6-0
at University of Texas L 10-18
at Texas A&M W 30-6
at Fort Worth University W 32-0

First Year Lettermen
C. I. Alexander, W. G. Carnahan, H. E. Field, G. A. Foote, S. S. Glasscock,
Guy Green, C. W. Herman, R. Holt, Guy Inman, Claude McClellan,
Jim V. McClintic, Frank Pruett, Sam Rutledge

1898 (1-3-1)*
University of Texas L 0-15
at Toby's Business College W 41-0
Fort Worth University T 0-0
at University of Texas L 0-29
Texas A&M L 0-16
*Colby Hall describes a snowy game in Midland,
without giving the opponent or the outcome.

First Year Lettermen
Lee Barron, C. E. Chambers, Colby D. Hall, John Montgomery,
James J. Ray, W. T. Watts, A. F. Wood, and J. N. Wooten
Second Year Lettermen
C. I. Alexander, W. G. Carnahan

1899 (0-0-1)
at Baylor T 0-0

First Year Lettermen
William Doherty, John Evans, Clovis Moore, Robert Moore,
William Moore, Wade Shumate, Charles Smith, Ted Smith
Second Year Lettermen
S. S. Glasscock, Colby D. Hall, James J. Ray

1900
NONE

1901 (1-2-1)
Taylor High School W 5-0
Baylor L 0-36
Trinity T 0-0
Baylor L 0-42

First Year Lettermen
Tom Reed
Third Year Lettermen
Clovis Moore, Wade Shumate

1902 (0-5-1)
Trinity University L 0-28
at Baylor T 0-0
Texas A&M L 0-22
Baylor L 0-6
at Trinity L 0-17
Baylor L 0-20

First Year Lettermen
Homer Rowe
Fourth Year Lettermen
Clovis Moore, Wade Shumate

1903 (0-6)
Baylor L 0-14
at Texas A&M L 6-22
at Trinity L 0-30
at Daniel Baker L 5-10
Texas A&M L 0-11
Baylor L 0-5
[Current media guides show an additional game with
Texas A&M, but records don't confirm this.]

First Year Lettermen
H. H. Watson
Fifth Year Lettermen
Clovis Moore, Wade Shumate

1904 (1-4-1)
Baylor T 0-0
at University of Texas L 0-40
at Fort Worth University L 0-4
at Texas A&M L 0-29
Baylor L 0-17
at Baylor W 5-0

First Year Lettermen
Charles Ashmore, Bertram Bloor, H. H. Bryant, Clyde
Burnett, Bonner Frizzell, John Garrard, I. C. Harbour, Howell
Knight, W. A. "Ambrosia" Martin, A. J. "The Heavenly"
Muse, Fred Obenchain, G. A. Wright, Pete Wright

1905 (4-4)
Baylor W 17-0
at University of Texas L 0-11
at Austin College W 21-0
at Texas A&M L 11-24
Baylor L 6-10
Trinity W 6-0
Texas A&M L 0-20
Baylor W 17-0

First Year Lettermen
W. M. Busy, T. B. Gallaher, Hardy Grissom, Dub Jones,
Jay McCullough, C. T. "Blue" Rattan, Wallace Wade
Second Year Lettermen
Howell Knight, W. A. "Ambrosia" Martin, A. J. "The Heavenly" Muse,
Bonner Frizzell, Charles Ashmore, Bertram Bloor, H. H. Bryant

1906 (2-5)
Fort Worth University L 0-6
at University of Texas L 0-22
at Texas A&M L 0-42
Texas A&M L 0-22
at Daniel Baker L 0-4
Deaf & Dumb Institute W 17-6
Fort Worth University W 9-5

First Year Lettermen
H. C. Barnard, Albert Billingsley, H. B. Dabbs, J. B. Frizzell,
Alex Howard, Noah C. "Cy" Perkins, John W. Pyburn,
Manley O. Thomas, Paul Tyson, J. O. Wallace

Second Year Lettermen
C. T. "Blue" Rattan
Third Year Lettermen
Pete Wright, H. H. Knight, W. A. Martin, Bonner
Frizzell, Bertram Bloor, H. H. Bryant

1907 (4-2-2)
at Fort Worth University T 0-0
at Baylor T 6-6
at Austin College W 27-0
at Trinity W 27-0
at Baylor W 11-10
at Texas A&M L 5-32
at Trinity W 6-5
at Baylor L 8-16

First Year Lettermen
Miles Bivins, B. F. Collins, Charles Fields, Ole Glover, A. M.
Harwood, William Massie, E. U. Scott, M. C. Stewart
Second Year Lettermen
Noah C. "Cy" Perkins, John W. Pyburn, Manley O. Thomas,
Paul Tyson, J. O. Wallace, Albert Billingsley
Third Year Lettermen
C. T. "Blue" Rattan, A. J. Muse
Fourth Year Lettermen
Pete Wright, Howell Knight, Bertram Bloor

1908 (6-3)
Deaf & Dumb Institute W 59-0
Baylor W 15-0
at University of Texas L 6-12
at Trinity W 11-10
Baylor W 10-6
Texas A&M L 10-13
Trinity W 22-0
at Southwestern W 14-0
Baylor L 8-23

First Year Lettermen
Marshall Baldwin, Miles Bevins, G. P. Braus,
Tom Lamonica, Morris Robison, Ray
Second Year Lettermen
William Massie, E. U. Scott, Miles Bivins, Charles Fields

Third Year Lettermen
Noah C. "Cy" Perkins, John W. Pyburn, Manley O. Thomas,
Paul Tyson, J. O. Wallace, Albert Billingsley
Fourth Year Lettermen
C. T. "Blue" Rattan, Bonner Frizzell, H. H. Bryant

1909 (5-2-1)
at Polytechnic W 42-0
at Texas A&M T 0-0
at Baylor W 9-0
at Austin College W 18-3
at University of Texas L 0-24
at Baylor W 11-0
at Southwestern W 12-0
at Baylor L 3-6

First Year Lettermen
Grantland Anderson, Edgar Bush, Milton Daniel,
William. V. Rattan, Aubel Riter
Second Year Lettermen
Y. Armen Yates, Marshall Baldwin, G. P. Braus, Tom Lamonica
Third Year Lettermen
William Massie, Charles Fields, Manley O. Thomas, Charles Ashmore
Fourth Year Lettermen
Paul Tyson, John W. Pyburn
Fifth Year Lettermen
C. T. "Blue" Rattan

1910 (2-6-1)
Polytechnic T 6-6
at Texas A&M L 0-35
at Baylor L 0-52
Trinity W 18-6
Texas A&M L 6-23
at Trinity W 9-0
at Southwestern L 3-25
Baylor L 3-10
Epworth L 0-30

First Year Lettermen
E. N. "Redwater" Anderson, Allen Freeman, Leon Gough, T. C. Graves,
Burl Hulsey, Henry G. Lavender, Ralph McCormick, Cecil Stiles, True
Strong, Clinton Swink, Oscar Wise, "Big" Mullican, Arthur Buster

Second Year Lettermen
Grantland Anderson, Edgar "Major" Bush,
Milton Daniel, William V. Rattan
Third Year Lettermen
Tom Lamonica
Fourth Year Lettermen
William Massie, Charles Fields (not a senior)

1911 (1-5)
Trinity W 30-0
at Southwestern L 0-21
at Austin College L 0-39
at Baylor L 0-12
Austin College L 8-18
Polytechnic L 3-16

First Year Lettermen
Clarence Bussey, John P. Cox, Ben Gantt, Allen Greeman, T. B. Hopkins,
Luther "Squabby" Parker, Grover W. Stewart, Bryan F. "Bun" Ware
Second Year Lettermen
Cecil Stiles, Henry G. Lavender, T. C. Graves,
E. N. "Redwater" Anderson, Allen Freeman
Third Year Lettermen
Milton Daniel

1912 (7-1)
at University of Texas L 10-30
at Southwestern W 20-0
Baylor W 22-0
at Austin College W 7-0
Polytechnic W 33-3
Howard Payne W 53-0
at Trinity W 48-13
Polytechnic W 21-7

First Year Lettermen
Charles Bassler, Oscar Golson, Hal Hunter, Joe McCullom,
Oran Osburn, Luke Ray, Ed Stewart, Jack Stratton, Alvin
Street, Lester Thannisch, J. H. J. Wallace, Charlie Walton
Second Year Lettermen
Luther "Squabby" Parker, Grover W. Stewart, Bryan F.
"Bun" Ware, Clarence Bussey, John P. Cox, Ben Gantt

Third Year Lettermen
Henry G. Lavender, Cecil Stiles, Allen Freeman, William V. Rattan

1913 (5-1-1)
Weatherford High T 0-0
Fort Worth YMCA W 32-6
Dallas W 3-0
at Howard Payne W 7-0
Fort Worth YMCA W 14-0
at Burleson College W 25-0
at Dallas L 0-6

First Year Lettermen
Jude Bivins, John Clark, Aaron Griffing, Lon Stewart,
Robert Waggaman, Raymond Fox, Joe McNamara,
Crawford B. Reeder (from Amarillo)
Second Year Lettermen
J. H. J. Wallace, Luke Ray, Alvin Street
Third Year Lettermen
Luther "Squabby" Parker, Ben Gantt
Fourth Year Lettermen
Allen Freeman

1914 (3-4-2)
North Texas State W 40-0
at Southwestern L 9-10
Oklahoma School of the Mines W 20-0
at Texas A&M L 0-40
at Rice Institute T 0-0
at Baylor L 14-28
Austin College W 13-0
at Daniel Baker L 0-33
at Howard Payne W 14-0
Trinity T 7-7

First Year Lettermen
John Anderson, Wilbur Brown, Ronald Garrett, W. B. Higgins,
Charles Hooper, Jesse Martin, Ewell McKnight, Clyde
Miller, John Nelson, Otis Ramsey, Howard Vaughn

Second Year Lettermen
Raymond Fox, Joe McNamara, Crawford Reeder

Third Year Lettermen
Alvin Street
Fourth Year Lettermen
Ben Gantt, John P. Cox, from Hillsboro

1915 (4-5)
at University of Texas L 0-72
SMU W 43-0
at Austin College W 28-0
Texas A&M L 10-13
at Rice L 3-33
at Trinity W 25-0
Southwestern W 21-0
Oklahoma A&M L 0-13
at Baylor L 0-51

First Year Lettermen
Aubrey Cook, Joe Edens, T. P. Frizzell, Abe Greines,
Alexander Kornegay, Ralph Martin, Edward Stangl
Second Year Lettermen
John Nelson, Otis Ramsey, Howard Vaughn, Jesse Martin, W. B. Higgins
Third Year Lettermen
Joe McNamara, Raymond Fox
Fourth Year Lettermen
John P. Cox (fifth year)

1916 (6-2-1)
at Meridian W 7-0
Austin College W 28-2
at SMU W 48-3
Rice T 7-7
Trinity W 35-0
at Southwestern L 13-14
at Daniel Baker W 23-0
at Howard Payne W 42-0
Baylor L 14-32

First Year Lettermen
Bill Berry, Cecil Bradford, Marion Broadley, Pug Calvert,
Gidden Culver, Astyanax Douglass, Criss Elliott, Froggie Hawes,
Dutch Meyer, Frank Ogilvie, Dave Tudor, Lee Willie
Second Year Lettermen
Joe Edens, Abe Greines, Alexander Kornegay,

Ralph Martin, Edward Stangl
Third Year Lettermen
John Nelson, Howard Vaughn

1917 (7-2)
Meridian College W 20-0
First Texas Artillery W 14-7
at Rice L 0-26
SMU W 21-0
at Trinity W 20-6
Southwestern W 20-6
Texas 141st Infantry L 7-14
at Austin College W 59-0
Baylor W 34-0
[Current media guides show an additional game with TCU
beating 111th Ambulance 6-0, but records don't confirm this.]

First Year Lettermen
Marion Brally, Loraine Dutton, Roy Graves, Joel Haden,
Tony (or William Troy Haire) Haire, Shadie Hale, Robert
Hogg, Calvin Kiker, Paul Lockman, J. M. Magill, Bryan
Miller, Heine Prinzing, Harold Sharpe, Houston Spikes
Second Year Lettermen
Froggie Hawes, Dutch Meyer, Cecil Bradford
Third Year Lettermen
Ralph Martin, Jesse Martin

1918 (4-3)
at University of Texas L 0-19
Carruthers Field L 6-7
at Southwestern W 14-6
at SMU (forfeit) L 0-1
Denton Normal W 39-0
Austin College W 25-0
at Baylor W 12-7

First Year Lettermen
Will Hill Acker, Bill Crunk, Jazz Cunningham, H. Hill, H. Jones, Ben
Parks, Scottie Rutherford, Ikey Sanders, Dave Singletary, Red Spiller
Second Year Lettermen
Bryan Miller, Joel Haden
Third Year Lettermen
Cecil Bradford

1919 (1-6)
Denton Normal L 6-14
Oklahoma A&M L 7-14
Southwestern L 0-10
at Trinity W 7-0
at Austin College L 0-6
Texas A&M L 0-48
Baylor L 0-7

First Year Lettermen
Chester "Boob" Fowler, Colvern Henry, Pud Hooser, Oscar Mayo,
Biss Newman, Roland "Cowboy" Ogan, Ray Smith, Vaughn Wilson
Second Year Lettermen
Red Spiller, Scottie Rutherford, Jazz Cunningham, Will Hill Acker
Third Year Lettermen
Joel Haden
Fourth Year Lettermen
Cecil Bradford

1920 (9-1)
Southeast Oklahoma W 20-0
Austin College W 9-7
at Arkansas W 19-2
at Trinity W 20-7
Phillips W 3-0
Missouri Osteopaths W 19-3
at Baylor W 21-9
Simmons College W 31-2
Southwestern W 21-16
Fort Worth Dixie Classic: 01/01 at Centre College L 7-63

First Year Lettermen
Melvin "Canuck" Bishop, Blair Cherry, Astyanax Douglass,
Pete Fulcher, Aubrey D. "Judge" Green, Wylie Harris,
Loren "Hootch" Houtchens, G. P. Jackson, Forrest Levy,
Bose McFarland, Allen Rowson, Raleigh "Rab" Ryan
Second Year Lettermen
Chester "Boob" Fowler
Third Year Lettermen
Red Spiller, Will Hill "Uncle Billy" Acker, Dutch Meyer

1921 (6-3-1)
West Texas State W 30-0
at Simmons College L 7-10
at Oklahoma A&M L 21-28
Trinity W 19-3
Tulsa University W 16-0
at Phillips University T 0-0
Missouri Osteopaths W 7-0
at SMU W 13-6
Haskell L 0-14
Arkansas W 19-14

First Year Lettermen
Homer Adams, Ivan Alexander, Hillard Camp, Ralph
Cantrell, Ashley "Fats" Crowley, Lindsey Jacks, Roy (Brick)
Largent, W. E. McConnell, E. G. Ohnsorg, W. M. Shirley
Second Year Lettermen
Raleigh "Rab" Ryan, Forrest Levy, Loren "Hootch" Houtchens,
Pete Fulcher, Aubrey D. "Judge" Green, Roland "Cowboy" Ogan
Third Year Lettermen
Melvin "Canuck" Bishop, Blair Cherry, Chester Fowler
Fourth Year Lettermen
Dutch Meyer

1922 (2-5-3)
at Dallas W 21-6
at Simmons T 7-7
Daniel Baker L 13-21
at Tulsa L 0-21
Oklahoma A&M W 22-14
at Austin College L 7-20
Howard Payne L 14-26
at Trinity T 7-7
at Kansas A&M L 0-45
SMU T 0-0

First Year Lettermen
Phillip Ayres, Kit Carson, Graham Estes, Dick Fender, Walter
Knox, Frank Stangl, Lawrence Tankersley, Pete Tomme
Second Year Lettermen
W. M. Shirley, W. E. McConnell, Lindsey Jacks, Homer
Adams, Ivan Alexander, Hillard Camp, Ralph Cantrell

Third Year Lettermen
Forrest Levy, Aubrey D. "Judge" Green, Melvin
"Canuck" Bishop, Roland "Cowboy" Ogan

NOTES

[1] Julia Kathryn Garrett, *Fort Worth: A Frontier Triumph* (Fort Worth: TCU Press, 1996), 290.

[2] Garrett records that the men repaired an existing structure.

[3] Garrett, *Fort Worth: A Frontier Triumph*, 337.

[4] Mark F. Bernstein, *Football: The Ivy League Origins of an American Obsession* (Philadelphia: University of Pennsylvania Press, 2001), 49.

[5] Theron J. Fouts, "The History and Influences of Football in Texas Colleges and Universities" (Masters Thesis, SMU, 1927), 16.

[6] "Athletics," the *Skiff*, September 26, 1902, 3.

[7] "He Tried To Explain Football," the *Skiff*, February 13, 1904.

[8] "Football Rules," the *Skiff*, January 7, 1905, 1.

[9] "Athletics," the *Skiff*, September 26, 1902, 3. Apparently the ladies obliged, and out-cheered the men, see the *Skiff*, October 4, 1902, 2.

[10] "Gridiron Gossip, Some Earnest Words from Coach Metzger," the *Lariat*, October 1, 1904.

[11] The *Campus*, October 8, 1918, 2.

[12] Colby D. Hall, *History of Texas Christian University: A College of the Cattle Frontier* (Fort Worth: TCU Press, 1947), 239.

[13] Mrs. Frank Miller Mason, "The Beginnings of Texas Christian University" (Masters Thesis, TCU, 1930), 38-40.

[14] *TCU Magazine*, September 1994, 50.

[15] Hall, *History of Texas Christian University*, 242.

[16] "Former Add Ran Football Star is Visitor Here," the *Skiff*, September 23, 1921, 1.

[17] The account taken from the *Horned Frog* in Hall, *History of Texas Christian University* claims that Add Ran was the first college team in Texas ever to score on the Longhorns; UT's own list of games and scores throws doubt on that claim. The TCU media guide and the UT list of all-time scores lists the score as 18-10, but the contemporary account given in the *Horned Frog*, and quoted by Colby D. Hall in his *History* gives 16-0. See www.mackbrown-texasfootball.com/sports/m-footbl/spec-rel/all-time-results.html.

[18] Hall, *History of Texas Christian University*, 244. Theron J. Fouts records the game scores and dates very differently, saying the Frogs played only Fort Worth University 1897, winning 32-0, and in 1898 playing Texas twice, losing 29-0 and 16-0, and Texas A&M once, losing 16-0. See Fouts's "History and Influence of Football in Texas Colleges and Universities," 113.

[19] Hall, 243.

[20] Ibid., 247-48.

[21] Ibid., 248.

[22] "Humiliating Defeat for Visiting Team—Score 36 to 0," the *Lariat*, November 30, 1901, 1.

[23] "Baylor vs. TCU," the *Skiff*, November 8, 1902.

[24] "Purple and White Defeated by A&M," the *Skiff*, November 22, 1902, 2.

[25] "Baylor vs. TCU," the *Skiff*, November 29, 1902.

[26] "Trinity vs. TCU," the *Skiff*, November 29, 1902, 2, 4.

[27] "Baylor Wins Series," the *Lariat*, December 6, 1902.

[28] "TCU Gets a Goose Egg," the *Lariat*, October 10, 1903, 1.

[29] "The Game," the *Skiff*, October 17, 1903, 1.

[30] "TCU Yells," the *Skiff*, September 22, 1906, 2.

[31]"Emory J. Hyde," the *Skiff*, September 29, 1906; "Varsity Enjoys a Tallyho Ride," the *Skiff*, November 4, 1907, 4.

[32] "Purple and White Invincible, Trounces Baylor Unmercifully in Spectacular Game Ending Sixteen to Nothing," the *Skiff*, October 2, 1905; "TCU Wins Game, Scores Three Touchdowns on Baylor in Opening Game," the *Lariat*, October 7, 1905; Theron J. Fouts records the score as 15-0 in his "History and Influence of Football in Texas Colleges and Universities," 113.
Lineup: LE Knight (Capt.); LT Muse; LG Owens; C Martin; RG Wright; RT Bloor; RE Frizzell; QB Grissom; LHB Ashmore; RHB Rattan; FB Gallaher. A pair of twins played at right guard for the Frogs, later in the season; they rotated at the A&M game, see "TCU Loses to A&M," the *Skiff*, November 6, 1905, 1.

[33]"Purple and White Invincible, Trounces Baylor Unmercifully in Spectacular Game Ending Sixteen to Nothing," the *Skiff*, October 2, 1905.

[34]"TCU Held Texas Down to 11-0," the *Skiff*, October 14, 1905, 1.

[35]"TCU is Victorious," the *Skiff*, November 6, 1905, 1.

[36] "TCU Loses to A&M," the *Skiff*, November 6, 1905, 1, 4.

[37] "Baylor Victorious, Defeats TCU 10 to 6 by Swift, Snappy, Superior Playing," the *Lariat*, November 17, 1905.

[38] "Baylor Snowed Under," the *Skiff*, December 2, 1905.

[39] John Sayle Watterson, *College Football: History, Spectacle, Controversy* (Baltimore: Johns Hopkins Universty Press, 2000), 102.

[40] "TCU Defeated By A&M," the *Skiff*, October 22, 1906, 1.

[41] Ibid.

[42] "One Remarkable Game," the *Skiff*, November 13, 1906, 1; "Daniel Baker Calls Off Game," the *Skiff*, November 26, 1906.

[43] "One Remarkable Game," the *Skiff*, November 13, 1906, 1.

[44]"Daniel Baker Calls Off Game," the *Skiff*, November 26, 1906.

[45]"TCU Defeats Baylor," the *Skiff*, October 22, 1909, 2.

[46]"Dummies Defeated, 33-0," the *Skiff*, October 14, 1907, 1.

[47]"TCU Loses to the Farmers," the *Skiff*, November 11, 1907, 1, 4.

[48]"Pete Wright Athletic Director Horned Frogs," the *Skiff*, September 19, 1922.

[49] "State Outplayed," the *Skiff*, October 14, 1908, 1.

[50]"Baylor Lost Championship," the *Lariat*, October 31, 1908.

[51]"Trinity Again," the *Skiff*, November 3, 1908, 1.

[52]"Trinity Is Bested," the *Skiff*, November 10, 1908, 1.

[53]"Baylor's Season Finishes In a Blaze of Glory!," the *Lariat*, November 28, 1908.

[54]"Thanksgiving Defeat," the *Skiff*, December 2, 1908, 1.

[55]Rick Waters, "A Fateful Fire," *TCU Magazine*, Spring 2010, 44.

[56]Or possibly merely panther tracks were seen at First and Throckmorton; or somewhere near where a big "Mexican Lion" had battered Parson Fitzgerald's dogs. For four different versions of the legend, see Oliver Knight, *Fort Worth: Outpost On the Trinity* (Norman: University of Oklahoma Press, 1953), 81-82.

[57]Watterson, *College Football: History, Spectacle, Controversy*, 120ff.

[58]"TCU Athletics, Entrance Requirements," the *Skiff*, August 19, 1910, 4.

[59]"A Hard Fought Game," the *Skiff*, November 16, 1911, 1.

[60]"Poly Is Very Easy Mark," the *Skiff*, October 31, 1912, 1.

[61]"There Is Something Wrong," the *Skiff*, April 24, 1913, 2.

[62]"Annual Baseball Banquet A Success," the *Skiff*, May 22, 1913, 1.

[63]"Athletics at TCU Not Dead," the *Skiff*, September 28, 1913.

[64]"TCU Warriors Overwhelmed By Husky A&M Team 40 to 0," the *Skiff*, October

16, 1914, 1, 4.

[65]"Interesting News Items From the Texas Schools," the *Lariat*, November 5, 1914, 3.

[66]"Completion of Proposed Athletic Field on Campus Will Make TCU A Center For High School Meets," the *Skiff*, October 29, 1915, 1.

[67]"Coaches Whipping Squad Into Shape, But Will Make No Promises," the *Skiff*, September 17, 1915, p. 4.

[68]"School Spirit Runs High At TCU and Freeland and Daniels Are Lauded," *Fort Worth Star-Telegram,* October 17, 1915, 19.

[69]"21-0," the *Skiff*, November 12, 1915, 1.

[70]"Athletic Material This Year Best in TCU Since 1912," the *Skiff*, August 11, 1916, 1.

[71]"Both Baylor and TCU Ready For the Big Game," the *Skiff,* November 24, 1916, 1.

[72]"Bears Victorious Over the Christians On Thanksgiving to Close Championship Season," the *Lariat*, December 7, 1916, 1.

[73]"TCU Pigskin Warriors Surprise On 'Dopesters,'" the *Skiff*, October 5, 1917, 1.

[74]"Christians Swamp Kangaroos, 59-0," the *Skiff*, November 23, 1917, 1.

[75]"Football Men Banqueted in Royal Style Wednesday Night," the *Skiff*, December 7, 1917, 4.

[76]"Was SMU Afraid?" the *Skiff*, November 2, 1918, 1.

[77]"*Horned Frogs* Lose Hard Fought Battle to Aggies, 14-7," the *Skiff*, October 22, 1919, 1, 3.

[78]"Rubenstein Pleads For More Pep," the *Skiff*, November 19, 1919, 1.

[79]"Bears Win Game By 7-0 Count," the *Skiff*, December 3, 1919, 1.

[80]"Baylor Loses to Horned Frogs at Cotton Palace Field," the *Lariat*, November 16, 1920, 3.

[81]"High Lights From the Baylor Game," the *Skiff*, November 19, 1920, 1.

[82]"TCU has More Pep for New Year's Game than for Season Games," the *Skiff*, December 20, 1920, 1.

[83]"Perfected TCU Defense May Surprise Colonels," *Dallas Morning News*, January 1, 1921.

[84]"TCU Eleven to Train at Canyon for Football," *Dallas Morning News*, July 1, 1921.

[85]"Public Primpers Duely [sic] Organized," the *Skiff*, October 10, 1922, 4.

[86] "Frogs Not to Shave Until They Win Game," *Dallas Morning News*, October 30, 1922.

[87] "Men Go Unshaven Until TCU Wins," the *Skiff*, October 31, 1922, 1.

[88] "TCU's Southwestern Athletics Conference Member Hereafter," the *Skiff*, December 12, 1922, 1.

[89] "Frogs Will Meet Mustangs," the *Skiff*, December 5, 1922, 1.

SOURCES CONSULTED

Bernstein, Mark F. *Football: The Ivy League Origins of an American Obsession*. Philadelphia: University of Pennsylvania Press, 2001.

Callaway, Rhonda L. "Hood County." *Handbook of Texas Online*. Published by the Texas State Historical Association. www.tshaonline.org/handbook/online/articles/hch17.

Fouts, Theron J. "The History and Influences of Football in Texas Colleges and Universities." Master's thesis, Southern Methodist University, 1927.

Garrett, Julia Kathryn. *Fort Worth: A Frontier Triumph*. Fort Worth: TCU Press, 1996.

Hall, Colby D. *History of Texas Christian University: A College of the Cattle Frontier*. Fort Worth: TCU Press, 1947.

Knight, Oliver. *Fort Worth: Outpost on the Trinity*. Norman: University of Oklahoma Press, 1953.

Mason, Mrs. Frank Miller. "The Beginnings of Texas Christian University." Master's thesis, Texas Christian University, 1930.

Paolantonio, Sal. *How Football Explains America*. Chicago: Triumph Books, 2008.

Pouncey, Temple. *Mustang Mania: Southern Methodist University*. Huntsville, Alabama: Strode Publishers, 1981.

Wallace, Patricia Ward. *Waco: Texas Crossroads*. Woodland Hills, California: Windsor Publications, 1983.

Wangrin, Mark. *Horns! A History: The Story of Longhorns Football*. New York: Touchstone/Fireside, 2006.

Watterson, John Sayle. *College Football: History, Spectacle, Controversy*. Baltimore: John Hopkins University Press, 2000.

2010 Horned Frog Football, TCU Football Media Guide

Baylor University's student newspaper, the *Lariat*

Census-year population figures for Texas counties are available at www.txcip.org/tac/census/CountyProfiles.php.

Fort Worth Record (newspaper—bought by the *Fort Worth Star-Telegram* in 1925)

SMU's student newspaper, the *Campus*

TCU's student newspaper, the *Skiff*

TCU Magazine

Dallas Morning News

INDEX

Calvert, Pug, 88-92, 94, 141
Camp Bowie, 95
Camp, Hillard, 124-126, 129, 143-144
Camp, Walter, 6, 8, 38, 103, 115
Cantrell, Ralph, 128, 143-144
Carlisle Military Academy, 67
Carnahan, W. G., 16, 133
Carruthers Field, 102, 141
Carson, Kit, 129-130, 144
Carter, Amon G., 60
Central (FW) High, 96, 112
Centre College, 114-115, 120-122, 126, 142
Cherry, Blair, 123, 125-129, 143
Chicago, University of, 8, 15
Cisco, TX, 69
Civil War, 1, 6
Clark, Addison, 1-5, 13-14, 16, 18-19
Clark, Addison "Little Addie," Jr., 14-15
Clark, Joseph Addison, 1-2
Clark, Randolph, 1-3
Clark, Sally McQuigg, 2
Columbia University, 6
Cox, John P., 67-72, 75, 79-87, 138-140
Cronk, C. E., 21, 27

Dabbs, H. B., 41, 135
Dalhart, TX, 112
Dallas Foot Ball Club, 8
Dallas Morning News, 108, 121
Dallas, TX, 2, 8-10, 16, 28, 32, 43, 47, 53, 55, 59-62, 69, 84-85, 88, 91, 103, 127-128, 131
Daniel Baker University, 26, 41-42, 82, 91-92, 128-129, , 134-135, 139-140
Daniel, Milton, 53, 55, 63-69, 84, 88-89, 91-92, 94, 98-100, 137-138
de Stivers, Cobby, 105, 108
Deaf & Dumb Institute, 42, 45, 48, 135-136
Denton Normal College (UNT), 103, 105, 141-142
Disciples of Christ Church, 18, 117
Douglass, Astyanax, 89, 91-92, 104, 112, 115, 118, 121, 126
Driver, Billy, 112, 116, 122, 124-127
Durant, OK, 115

Easley, A. C., 8, 14-15, 100
Edens, Joe, 85-87, 89-92, 94, 140-141
Epworth University, 60, 66, 137

Fair Park, Dallas, 28, 85, 91
Field, H. E., 16, 133
Field, Joe Y., 16
Fields, Charles, 46, 55, 63-66, 68, 136-138
First Texas Artillery, 95, 141
Flying Wedge, 7, 11

Foote, G. A., 16, 19, 133
Forney, TX, 62
Fort Worth, 1-4, 8-9, 53, 59-63, 65-66, 68, 71-72, 75, 77, 79, 82, 86-88, 92-93, 97-98, 100, 103, 107-108, 112, 114-115, 117-118, 120-125, 128-129, 131-132
Fort Worth and Denver Railroad, 128
Fort Worth Heavyweights, 8
Fort Worth University Packers, 8, 16, 19, 28, 39, 42-43, 60, 66, 133, 135-136
Fowler, Chester, 105, 107, 109, 112, 116, 118, 120-126, 142
Fox, Ray, 79, 84-85, 139-140
Freeland, E. Y., 84, 88
Frizzell, Bonner, 28-29, 36, 38, 40-43, 48, 53, 135-137, 140
Frizzell, J. B., 48, 53
Fulcher, Pete, 112, 117, 143

Gainesville, TX, 59
Gallaher, T. B., 32, 34-36, 135
Gantt, Ben, 79, 81, 138-140
Georgetown, TX, 51, 65, 68, 70, 80, 91
Glasscock, S. S., 16, 133
Golson, Oscar, 69, 139
Granbury, TX, 3
Granger, TX, 112
Graves, Roy, 99, 141
Graves, T. C., 68, 138
Green, Guy, 16, 133
Green, Judge, 116, 126, 143
Greenville, TX, 78
Greines, Abe, 84, 90, 93-94, 140-141
Grissom, Napoleon, 24, 27-28, 32, 35, 54, 135
Gumm, C. C., 74, 82

H&TC. Southland line, 86
Hackney, T. E. D., 104, 106, 110
Haden, Joel, 100, 106-107, 108, 141-142
Haire, Troy, 97, 100-101, 112, 117, 141
Hall, Colby D., 17, 59, 133
Hamner, Professor, 21-22
Hanna, John, 1
Harbour, I. C., 29, 135
Harris, Walter "Wylie," 116, 118, 120, 143
Harvard University, 6, 37, 114
Harwood, A. M., 41, 46, 136
Haskell College, 125, 143
Hawes, Denton "Froggie," 84, 90, 94, 97, 99, 101, 141
Hell's Half Acre, 2
Henry, Colvern, 112, 142
Herring, C. W., 16
Hildebrand, H. E., 21-22
Hillsboro, TX, 67, 140
Holt, R., 16, 133
Honey, Bill, 124, 127-129

Hooser, Pud, 107-108, 142
Houston Heavyweights, 16, 133
Houston Post, 98
Houston, TX, 16, 81, 86, 133, 141
Houtchens, Loren, 112, 118, 124-125, 127, 143
Howard Payne University, 71, 77-78, 82, 91-92, 129, 138-140, 143
Hyde, Emory J., 32, 34, 36, 38-39, 43, 47, 56, 70, 94

Jackson, Gilbert P., 112, 116, 118, 120-122, 127, 143
Jarrott, J. E., 3
Jarvis, Ida Van Zandt, 2
Jarvis, Van Zandt, 94

Kansas A&M (Kansas State), 131, 143
Katy Railway, 48
Knight, Howell, 32, 37-40, 42-46, 48-50, 53, 135-136
Kornegay, Ox, 89-92, 140-141

Lamonica, Tom, 55-56, 58, 67-68, 136-138
Langley, J. R., 47, 53-54, 56
Lariat, the [Baylor Univ.], 21-22, 24-25, 34, 36, 50, 52-53, 66, 92, 104, 110, 118-119
Lavender, Henry, 63, 69, 138-139
Lever, Henry, 66-67, 69
Lewis, Kemp, 62, 65
Livsey, Doc, 127
Lockhart, Clinton, 58
Lockman, Paul, 95-99, 101, 112, 141

Manhattan, KS, 131
Martin, Jesse, 79, 82
Martin, Ralph "Gish," 83-84, 87-95, 98, 140-141
Martin, W. A. "Ambrosia," 29, 38, 135-136
mass plays, 8, 37, 61
Massie, William, 44-45, 47-51, 54-56, 62, 65-66, 136-138
Mayo, Oscar, 107-108, 112, 116, 142
McClellan, Claude, 16, 133
McClintic, Jim V., 16, 19-20, 133
McCormick, Ralph, 62, 64-65, 138
McCullum, Joe, 70, 139
McGill University, 6
McKee, Frank, 84
McKinney, TX, 59, 62
McKnight, Ewell, 82, 140
McKnight, John, 112, 122, 127-128, 131
McMillin, Bo, 115, 121-122
McNamara, Joe, 76-77, 79-80, 84, 139-140
Melton, Carl, 58
Meridian College, 95-96, 141
Methodist Female College, 4-5
Meyer, Dutch, 89-92, 94, 97, 99, 101, 104, 112, 114-115, 117-118, 122, 132,

141, 143
Michigan, University of, 14
Miller, Bryan, 95-103, 112, 141-142
Miller, Clyde, 79
Milwee, Edwin, 4
Mineral Wells, TX, 79
Missouri Osteopaths, 118, 123-124, 142-143
Moore, Clovis, 24-25, 133-134
Mullican, "Big," 54-55, 138
Muse, A. J., 21-28, 32, 34-36, 135-136
Muse, the younger, 43, 45

Nelson, John C., 80, 84, 86, 89-94, 140-141
Newman, Biss, 106, 108, 142
North Side (FW) High School, 84, 89, 112, 115
North Texas State Normal College (UNT), 79, 103

Obenchain, Fred, 25, 29, 32, 43, 135
Odeon (cinema), 61
Ogan, Roland "Cowboy," 105-107, 109, 112, 116, 122, 124-125, 127-128, 142-144
Ogilvie, Frank, 91, 94, 104
Oklahoma A&M, 49, 81, 87, 106-107, 123, 128-129, 140, 142-143
Oklahoma School of the Mines, 80, 139

Padgitt's Park, 19
Panic of 1873, 4, 60
Parker, Luther "Squabby," 69, 76-77, 80, 138-139
Parks, Ben, 4, 100, 103, 142
Pennsylvania, University of, 6
Perkins, Noah C. "Cy," 38-43, 45, 47-53, 135-137
Phillips University, 117-118, 123, 142-143
Polytechnic University, 8, 53-54, 63, 68-69, 71-72, 74, 79, 137-138
Princeton, 6-7, 9
Prinzing, Heine, 95-96, 99, 104, 112, 122, 141
Pruett, Frank, 16, 133
Public Primpers, 126
Pulitzer, Joseph, 6, 12
Pyburn, John, 41, 43-44, 47-48, 53-56, 135-137

Ramsey, Otis, 79-81, 84, 86-87, 140
Rattan, C. T. "Blue," 32, 38, 48, 53, 55, 63, 65, 70-73, 135-137
Ray, Luke, 75, 139
Reeder, Crawford B., 77-82, 139-140
Rice Institute, 81, 84, 86, 91, 96, 127, 139-141
Robertson, Julia Easley, 15
Rogers, Dan, 103
Roosevelt, Teddy, 1
Rowe, Homer, 22, 24, 26-27, 134
Rowson, Allen, 116-119, 121, 143
Rugby, 6
Rutgers University, 6

ABOUT THE AUTHOR

Ezra Hood graduated from TCU's music school in 2005, shortly after marrying his sweetheart and fellow Horned Frog Shannon. He has followed and written about TCU football ever since. He is a lawyer for his day job in Fort Worth. The Hoods raise a growing family of native Frog fans in Dallas.